CELEBRATE
JESUS

CELEBRATE JESUS

The Stories Behind
Your Favorite Praise
and Worship Songs

PHIL CHRISTENSEN and SHARI MACDONALD

Kregel
Publications

*Celebrate Jesus: The Stories Behind Your Favorite Praise
and Worship Songs*

© 2003 by Phil Christensen and Shari MacDonald

Published by Kregel Publications, a division of Kregel, Inc.,
P.O. Box 2607, Grand Rapids, MI 49501. Kregel Publications
provides trusted, biblical publications for Christian growth and
service.

Scripture quotations marked KJV are from the King James Version of the Holy Bible.

Scripture quotations marked New Living Translation are from
the *Holy Bible, New Living Translation,* Copyright © 1996.
Used by permission of Tyndale House Publishers, Inc.,
Wheaton, IL 60189. All rights reserved.

Library of Congress Cataloging-in-Publication Data
Christensen, Phil, and MacDonald, Shari
    Celebrate Jesus: the stories behind your favorite praise
and worship songs / [edited] by Phil Christensen and Shari
MacDonald.
        p.   cm.
    1. Hymns, English—History and criticism. I. Christensen,
Phil. II. MacDonald, Shari.
BV315.C45   2003   264'.23—dc21   2003009057
                                                                            CIP
ISBN 0-8254-2381-3

Printed in the United States of America

2 3 4 5 / 07 06 05 04 03

Contents

PREFACE

We live in a scientific age, an age of reason. In theory, most questions can be answered simply by gathering data: Who was the inventor of Velcro? What is the square root of 127,893,435,204? How does photosynthesis occur? Therefore, it seems perfectly reasonable to ask (and to expect to find an answer to) the question: *What inspires the creation of today's most popular praise and worship songs?*

There are, of course, various answers. And the authors of this volume (scientific souls that we are) have sought to provide some of the reasons in these pages.

The stories in which these answers are found are, we believe, thoroughly fascinating. You will meet a contemporary Christian music star who wrote out of pure obedience while in a deep spiritual funk. Another, a spiritually dry worship leader, cried out to God for a deeper relationship with Him. A bleary-eyed Christian recording artist made up a tune to help him keep his eyes open during a late-night road trip; and a young, itinerant preacher called on the Lord to provide financially for his family.

There is the church music director who was determined to write an uplifting anthem for a children's Easter musical, as well as the teenage girl from southern California who wrote a now-classic worship song while on the way home from the beach.

These and other stories help us know just a little more about the nature of God, and they inspire us to respond to Him. The stories are as varied as the songwriters themselves.

As you read these stories, we hope that you will be amazed at God's goodness, at the myriad ways He works in the lives of His people, at His ability to redeem even the darkest circumstance, and at His daily miracles.

Of course, when miracles occur, it is human nature to want to know their cause, so that we can make them happen again. As these stories unfold, new questions may arise:

What makes a classic worship song work?

What do these songs have in common?

What traits do they share?

If we can determine the answers to such questions, perhaps we can create as many highly singable praise and worship songs as we desire, a library of songs like "Draw Me Close," "My Tribute," and "Awesome God." Perhaps this is what the music executive had in mind when he told Michael Kelly Blanchard, in all seriousness: "I just want you to write me another 'Be Ye Glad.'"

If only it were so easy! How handy it would be if we could all plunk ourselves down at the piano or sequester ourselves away in a quiet corner and pen a "My Redeemer Lives," an "Only by Grace," or a "Come, Let Us Worship and Bow Down" any time we pleased.

At the same time, how dull it would be if there were dozens or hundreds of the same sort of song, each born a similar way. The monotony of them would put our spirits to sleep, rather than stir us to praise. How much more exciting it is to wonder, *Where will God move next?* and *How?* and *Through whom?* And, perhaps best of all, *What will He have to say this time?*

As you read through the stories in this book, you will perhaps be struck by several similarities in the accounts. You may notice how often the songwriter offers in astonishment, even years after the fact, some variation of the claim: "I didn't feel as though *I* wrote the song at all!"

At the same time, each song story is wonderful and unique. Pinning down the creation—or the Creator—is like trying to tack a breeze to the wall. Impossible—and who would want to, in any case? We have every reason to be thankful that it cannot be done. After all, it is this very unpredictability, the very necessity of God's intervention, that makes the creation of enduring praise and worship songs so miraculous, so worthy of our surprise, admiration, and joy.

Michael Kelly Blanchard, author of "Be Ye Glad," put it this way during an interview with Phil Christensen, not long after Michael had watched the Grammy Awards on television:

> I have seen enough of those shows to know that there is a great tendency with them to want to freeze every aspect of something that has become beloved. However, frequently God's style is *not* to work that way. He's the long-awaited Messiah who shows up in a smelly little, back-alley barn when no one is looking. That is indicative of how things so often work with God: He just picks His own time and His own agenda. The best we can do for that is gratitude.

Indeed, each person profiled in this book is unique. Each song plays a different part in God's great story. And each individual story offers its own glorious testimony to God's heart and to the fulfillment of His purposes. For these glimpses, and for the songwriters who shared them with us, we are profoundly grateful.

As was the case with our first volume, *Our God Reigns: The Stories Behind Your Favorite Praise and Worship Songs*, released in 2000, Phil and I are indebted to the modern-day psalmists who shared their experiences with us. Every possible effort was made to run the stories by them for final verification; in the rare instances where this was not possible, we relied on our interview notes for accuracy. To each of these men and women, we offer sincere thanks. Chatting with you has been, in the truest sense, a little slice of heaven.

To Jim Kregel, Dennis Hillman, Steve Barclift, Janyre Tromp, and Wendy Yoder at Kregel Publications—each one the very picture of patience and graciousness, as well as a genuine friend—we also offer our deepest thanks. I offer sincere personal thanks to them and to the rest of the faithful Kregel crew, who in spring 2002 joined my friends and family in praying me through a life-threatening case of pneumonia, an illness that ultimately delayed the completion and publication of this volume (although none of these folks ever pressured me or complained). Every writer knows that it is wonderful to have a company that cares about your book. But it is a vastly greater blessing to have a publishing house that cares about your life.

Phil and I also extend our sincere appreciation to Dave Gauthier and Marilyn Bailiff at CCLI for helping us contact many of these wonderful songwriters, and to Ginny Elliott and Linda Boatman for providing assistance in getting their stories onto the page.

I am especially thankful to my coauthor and former youth pastor and music minister, Phil Christensen, for helping to instill in me a deep love for God when I was still wearing braces, and for inviting me along on the song story ride.

And to you, the reader: May the following pages truly bring glory to God, reveal some aspect of His character you've never seen before, and help to deepen your love and devotion to Him.

—SHARI MACDONALD

1

ALMIGHTY

WAYNE WATSON

"It didn't start out as a praise song. It started off as a reluctant act of obedience."

Little did his audiences know that Wayne Watson's faith was being sorely tested.

In the early 1990s, Wayne Watson was at the height of his career in Christian music ministry. Known for such classic albums as *Watercolor Ponies* and such standout contemporary songs as "For Such a Time As This," he was one of Christian music's rising stars. Wayne packed auditoriums with men, women, teens, and children who were excited to hear him testify in song about God's goodness, as well as about his own faith.

With a successful eighteen-year marriage to his wife, Lynn; a teenage son, Neal; a preteen son, Adam; and a growing music ministry, Wayne appeared to have it all. Yet behind the scenes, he was struggling through one of the hardest times of his life.

"Our family had just lost a very close friend, Sandra, to leukemia," Wayne says. "She fought it for almost a year. She was a dear young lady with four young daughters. To be honest, heaven was somewhat silent to me at that time."

It was a time when prayers seemed to "bounce off the ceiling," with "not much coming back."

"I was spiritually stuck," he explains. "I didn't know how to get out of it. Then one night I felt as if the Holy Spirit was directing me to confess that He is God, and I am not. I was just to believe—and to believe that He *always* would be sovereign—even though I didn't feel like it."

Wayne sat down at the piano and obeyed. The result is the praise and worship song "Almighty."

"The song flowed once I got started," Wayne recalls. "It seemed almost like the lyrics wrote themselves. There are songs that take weeks and sometimes years to write. Sometimes they have to sit and age for a season—or two or three—and then I feel like they're ready to be recorded or written. But this one happened relatively quickly.

"Although Christians today sing 'Almighty' as a worship song of praise, singing it at first was more an act of obedience than inspiration. The song was a confession that God was in charge. He would reveal Himself in His time, not in mine. I said the things in the song out of an obedient heart."

God used this act of obedience as part of the process of healing Wayne's wounded heart. "I believe that it helped me get a better perspective on my life and upon the ageless faithfulness of God. In time—probably a longer time than I would have liked—after believing the lyrics of the song and silently singing and praying them to myself, I came out of that period of spiritual struggle. But it did take time."

The song was so personal, in fact, that it almost was never heard beyond the walls of Wayne's house.

"The producer that I was working with at the time [on the album *Home Free*] and the head of the record company that I was with [Word] came to my house in Houston to listen to the songs that I'd written for this album. There were maybe twelve or fourteen songs on this tape. I hate to sit and listen with people as they're listening to my stuff. I can't even describe how embarrassing it is sometimes, because I really hope they like my work. I'm sitting there being scrutinized, revealing my 'babies' to somebody for the first time. I hope they don't say that they're ugly.

"I gave them the cassette and I said, 'Here are the songs I've been working on for six months. I'm going to leave the room now, and I'm going to let you guys listen to these songs. There's one on here that I absolutely don't want to record, but I left it on the tape anyway. It's called "Almighty." It's different from anything I've ever done, and I don't think it should be on the record.'"

With that, Wayne walked out of the room.

"Because it was very personal, I didn't know if it was good musically or not. I haven't written much praise and worship music. I wish I had written more, because this has reached a lot of people, and a lot of people sing it in their churches. I wish I had more of that in me. I wish I could make myself do it, but I just can't. This one came from a unique situation."

The two men listened to Wayne's tape and immediately saw the potential in "Almighty." They came out of the room and said, "You're crazy. You *will* record this."

In the months that followed, Wayne played "Almighty" every night in concert. Word Music made efforts to introduce the song through choral arrangements and various other recordings. "Little by little," Wayne says, "people absorbed it and embraced it. I was surprised. I'd go places and start to play it, and the audience would start singing it. It just blew me away."

The song quickly became one of the most popular praise and worship songs in contemporary churches and remains so today.

A decade after writing it—and two decades after entering music ministry—Wayne is still a popular Christian artist, and he continues to sing "Almighty" at each performance. "I've opened my concerts with it for several years now, because it seems to set the tone. From the very first note, you don't have to wonder, *Is this a Christian song or is this not a Christian song?* That's what I like about it: It's very obvious."

Despite his broad influence as a writer and performer in contemporary Christian music, Wayne realizes that he probably will be remembered most for "Almighty."

"My mom thinks I've made it because I'm in the hymnbook," he laughs, "so everything else is downhill!"

Story approved by Wayne Watson.

2

Ancient of Days

JAMIE HARVILL AND GARY SADLER

"It's something people have asked us to duplicate. I say, 'You're crazy!' Lightning never strikes twice in the same place."

Ancient of Days" is one of those praise songs that worship leaders prize like gold.

The magic of the piece lies, in part, in its creative marriage between the subject of God's mystery and the tangible South African-style rhythms. But far more goes on in the song than first meets the ear. In a joyful, multicultural explosion of praise, the lyrics—like Scripture text on which it is based—blend the transcendence of the Eternal One with the immanence and everlasting reign of His Son.

In its full impact, "Ancient of Days" really rocks the flock.

Throughout the brief history of modern praise and worship music, worship artist Ron Kenoly's recordings have introduced terrific songs, such as "Mourning into Dancing" and "High Places," into the larger church-body's lexicon of praise. In 1991, the song "Ancient of Days" joined this illustrious company after Kenoly's *Lift Him Up* album included a seven-minute arrangement, modeled with a brass set up and Abraham Laboriel's stunning bass solo.

That recording effectively launched Jamie Harvill as a writer of praise songs, as well as the careers of co-writer and friend Gary Sadler. At the time, Jamie was thirty years old, but he'd been headed for a songwriting career his entire life.

As a youth in Fullerton, California, Jamie grew up in the original hometown of Fender guitars, listening to the Beatles, the Beach Boys, and early AM radio.

"Early on," he says, "I caught a real understanding and was able to identify with pop music because it cut to the chase in its ability to give a message in three minutes.

"When I was about twelve, I realized that I belonged to that musical world. Although I wasn't a Christian at the time, I felt like my musical talents were developing and I started to see that I was good at it."

Jamie began to play lead and rhythm guitar, and enjoyed playing both electric and acoustic. It was, however, the folk-rock songwriters of the 1970s, like Cat Stevens and America, who truly captured young Jamie's imagination. "The lyrics and music did more for me than the whole rock and roll thing. I identified with the singer/songwriters early on."

Young Jamie wrote his first song, "Albatross," when he was just thirteen.

"In school, I'd read about a lone bird that flew on its own. I was interested in that, because I felt like I was flying on my own and maybe someday I'd find a place."

A friend and neighbor who was involved in Satanism offered Jamie just such a place of acceptance, and for a time, Jamie also dabbled in the occult. But, in an ironic twist, these experiences ultimately led him back to the truth.

"It helped me to think about heaven and hell. It also helped me to think, *If the Devil is real then maybe there's a real God. . . .*"

These epiphanies, combined with a godly, praying grandmother; early childhood experiences at a vacation Bible school; and, finally, the emotional impact of an Easter musical, led Jamie Harvill to commit his life to Christ in April of 1975.

Now a talented young musician *and* a Christian, Jamie soon found himself at ground zero of what would one day be called the worship movement. This occurred at Calvary Chapel in Costa Mesa, where on a weekly basis he looked up to—and was highly influenced by—seminal artists like Keith Green, The Way, and Mustard Seed Faith.

"I was only a fifteen/sixteen-year-old worship groupie at that time!" he says. "It was the beginning of worship music as we know it today. Jesus, music, and my culture all came together in southern California in 1975 to 1976."

Jamie's musical experiences in the following years included a three-year stint with the band Truth. Already a fine performer, Jamie developed a deeper understanding of Christian music during his time with the group. "I had learned a lot of things musically, but then I went into Truth and I learned some more important things. Greater things, like how to minister in churches and denominations. It gave me a love for the local church."

He later got off the road and enrolled in college in Mobile, Alabama. There, he married Brenda, who he'd met while on tour. He also began a relationship with Integrity Music, which was being launched in Mobile at that time.

Jamie's talent quickly brought him to the attention of Vice President Don Moen and others at the fledgling organization. Once again, he was at ground zero of a new worship movement. Songwriter Gerrit Gustafson, part of the early creative team at Integrity, was among those who had faith in Jamie. One day Gerrit said, "Jamie, I know you're wanting to make it in songwriting and I want to be the first one to invest in it." He handed Jamie $100 and said, "Buy your four-track [recorder]."

"I matched the money," says Jamie, "and bought the four-track that we later did this demo of 'Ancient of Days' on."

At this point in Jamie's life, he also reconnected with an old friend, Gary Sadler, who he'd met years before while still touring.

"We'd said that one day we'd write a song together," says Jamie. When the two hooked up again, Jamie found Gary at loose ends, but ready to write.

"Gary had just lost his job at a manufacturing plant. He said he didn't know what he wanted to do with his life, but he did want to write songs. I said, 'Let's write them together.'

"So Gary and his family came down to our three-bedroom, one-bath, small house, with his two kids and wife. We set up a demo studio in my son's room. We kicked him out. Gary had an idea with a rhythm and I was playing with some African rhythms. We got together and collaborated on these musical ideas.

"Lyrically, we settled on Daniel chapter 7, where it talks about being around the throne and how we can experience that now. We put this song together and demoed it on the four-track."

Marty Nystrom, then Director of Song Development at Integrity, loved "Ancient of Days" and knew it was right for the upcoming Ron Kenoly recording. Integrity also used the song to broaden the focus of its arrangements; "Ancient of Days" was the first of the company's recordings to feature musicians—not just vocalists—as worshipers.

Jamie, who had been very fond of Kenoly's work, attended the recording session. "I drove down with my parents and two children to the recording, and before our eyes we saw 'Ancient of Days' come alive. I heard it and it was almost like God touched me on the shoulder and said, 'This is hot!' My mother and father looked at me and said, 'Look out. This is good.'"

Shortly after, Integrity signed both Jamie and Gary as staff writers. Jamie has since penned such standards as "Firm Foundation" and "Because We Believe," and Gary has also written many songs, including "Lord, I Thirst for You" and the lovely "Be Unto Your Name" with Lynn DeShazo. Both Jamie and Gary have been featured on numerous projects, including those in Integrity's powerful Songwriters' Series.

Looking back at the success of "Ancient of Days," Jamie smiles. "It's something people have asked us to duplicate, and I look at them and say, 'You're crazy!' Lightning never strikes twice in the same place. But the song gave Gary and me a platform from which to do what God created us to do."

For Jamie, that work includes serving in the local church, which he has continued to hold in high regard since traveling with Truth.

In addition to his songwriting career, he leads worship at True Life Church in Franklin, Tennessee, where nationally known youth speaker, author, and radio host Dawson McAllister is pastor. Jamie also owns his own worship resource company, designed to help small churches revitalize their worship.

"Being in a local church *is* the highest calling," he says. "It's not 'out there somewhere.' In other words, what God has given to me in my hands is the highest musical calling I could ever have. It's what we were meant to do—to worship God. People need to stop looking for something greater, because we're already in the greatest place with the local church.

"Songs are just tools to get people closer to God," he says with confidence. "That's all there is to it. That's why I continue to write, to put into three minutes a lot of stuff that will draw people close to God."

Story approved by Jamie Harvill.

3

Awesome God

RICH MULLINS

"Rich never really thought it was that great of a song."

On September 19, 1997, contemporary Christian music lost one of its favorite sons. Rich Mullins, acclaimed songwriter and singer, was traveling to Kansas to participate in a benefit concert for a missions program. Late that evening on a highway near Peoria, Illinois, Rich was killed in a car accident. Well loved before his death, Rich is today nothing less than a modern day legend, inspiring awe, devotion, admiration, and a deeper love for God in fans old and new.

One of the most colorful and honest figures in Christian music, Rich was known for a wide range of qualities and quirks: from his dark, oddball humor to his devotion to the teachings of St. Francis of Assisi; from his legendary temper tantrums to his heart for youth; from his tendency to forget song lyrics on stage to his down-in-the-trenches compassion for Native Americans. And his music. Always his music.

Four days after his death, *The Daily Mississippian* called Rich "the undisputed most prolific songwriter in Christian music." Indeed, Rich was the author of some of Christian music's most famous and enduring tunes, including "Sing Your Praise to the Lord," "If I Stand," "Creed," and "Hold Me, Jesus." But perhaps none of his songs is more beloved than the widely sung "Awesome God."

The story of the song's origination is recalled by Kathy Sprinkle, a long-time friend of Rich. Kathy met Rich on her first day at Cincinnati Bible College, where he was also attending. She remained friends with Rich throughout his life, and last spoke with him the day before his death.

Kathy says that Rich was never excited about sharing how "Awesome God" was born.

"He would say in concert, 'Everybody wants to know how I wrote this song, and I'm really embarrassed, because the story isn't real spiritual or anything.'

"He was driving across country," says Kathy. "We're from the Independent Christian Churches, and we have a big sing—Christ in Youth Conference—in the summertime at different college campuses. Rich was going to a CIY conference. He had a little teeny Ford Ranger truck, and he was trying to pull this big U-Haul trailer full of music equipment with it. The truck wouldn't go more than like fifty miles an hour.

"He was going from Missouri to Colorado and it's all uphill. People think Kansas is flat, but it does eventually go up, and the truck wouldn't pull."

Along the way, Rich needed a way to keep himself awake.

"It was sort of a joke that Rich got more sleep behind the wheel of the car than he got in bed. He had a tendency to fall asleep behind the wheel. He was trying to keep himself awake and he started telling himself a story from the Scriptures."

Fortunately, Rich's bizarre sense of humor provided the inspiration he needed to stay awake.

"Rich had this habit of doing a black Baptist preacher thing," says Kathy. "So he started talking to himself, doing that rhythm thing that a lot of inner-city black pastors do: 'Huh *dah*, dah *dah*, dah dah *dah*.' And he preached to himself out loud. He told stories to himself—stories about the Scriptures—and ended up writing a song. That's how 'Awesome God' got born."

But, says Kathy, "He never thought it was that great of a song."

Upon his arrival in Colorado, Rich taught the song to the youth at the conference. The kids took the song away from the gathering. Soon youth groups everywhere were sharing it with their home congregations.

"The kids at CIY did this song probably three years before Rich put it on an album project," says Kathy. "Everybody already knew it by the time it was on the record."

Rich's label initially was uncertain about a portion of the song's lyrics. "They didn't like 'When he rolls up his sleeves he ain't just puttin' on the Ritz.' They thought it was disrespectful. But the kids liked the thought of God rolling up his sleeves. And Rich said, 'But it says in the Scriptures that "he bared his holy arm!"'" Rich was a very interesting character, that's for sure!" Kathy laughs.

Rich's favorite song of his own, Kathy recalls, was "Elijah," written in the early 1980s.

"He wrote 'Elijah' right after John Lennon died—John Lennon was this huge idol of Rich's. It was also right around the time that Rich's great-grandmother died. She'd had more effect on Rich than anybody else—as far as his Christian walk and believing in him. She was a great old lady, and he thought how sad it was that his great-grandma had done so many wonderful things for the world, and nobody would ever know about her. And it was pretty questionable whether John Lennon had ever done anything that was really that great, and everybody was bemoaning his death.

"It was the first time," says Kathy, "that Rich realized, 'Someday I'm going to die.' He wrote that song as his own epitaph, to say, 'I have to accept the fact that I'm going to die someday. I'm going to continue to sing this song and live my life as though I understand that I'm going to die, and I need to live my life the way I need to live it.' That was his song."

One of Rich's most enduring legacies is his work with Native Americans. In the mid-1990s, Rich left his home in Nashville to move to Kansas, where he ministered extensively on the reservation. A great portion of Rich's time and resources were focused on this work, and years after his death, his work there continues.

After the accident, Rich's mother dedicated his finances to start a foundation for continuing his work on the reservations. The foundation, called The Legacy, is today led by Rich's brother, David Mullins, and run by a group of Rich's friends and associates, who remain close to his work. The royalties from Rich's music all go to

The Legacy, including those from some of Rich's previously un-published work.

"Rich died with about eighty songs that were unpublished. We started a publishing company, Mullinsongs," says Kathy. "We just sold one song to Caedmon's Call, and I'm working with some other people to get other songs sold. Some of them are really good; some of them are self-indulgent memories of a nineteen-year-old. We're still working with all that stuff."

The work of The Legacy provides for missionaries, suicide prevention counseling, and leadership training on a number of reservations. It also funds a unique type of art music camp, which includes instruction in art, guitar, hammer dulcimer, banjo, and percussion, as well as drama performance.

"What we do is not that great," Kathy says humbly, "and for some reason, God shows up and does these amazing things. We believe that the natives have been too many people's projects. So our whole idea is to teach art and music with no other agenda. They know we're Christians, and God always opens the doors for amaz-ing things. Kids right and left decide to think again about what they call 'the white man's God.'"

Today, Rich's loss is still felt keenly by those who loved him.

"When Rich would write a song, he'd get so excited about it," recalls Kathy. "He would do things like call you at three o'clock in the morning and make you listen to his songs. What I wouldn't give to have that back again! I would never begrudge him getting me up at three o'clock in the morning, that's for sure."

Yet many find solace in knowing that the ministry he loved still prospers. A social worker, Kathy finds satisfaction in seeing Rich's work on the reservations live beyond him.

"It's fun for me to see Rich's dream keep happening," she says. "It's wonderful."

Story approved by Kathy Sprinkle.

4

Awesome in This Place

DAVE BILLINGTON

"I sometimes wonder if it may have been popular in heaven. Perhaps it was declining on the charts, and they wanted to try it out in a new market. You know how things go after thousands of years. . . ."

Many of God's children know: Being in a spiritual desert can leave a person feeling incredibly dry.

It can also create a thirst for God that only He can quench, driving us to Him, ultimately leading us to blessings and bringing Him tremendous glory. This is a lesson that Dave Billington, an experienced songwriter, learned over a period of several years.

Years ago, at the beginning of a new year, a few words bubbled to the surface of Dave's mind, forming part of what he thought could very well be a song. But the rest of the lyric fell out of reach, then drifted away.

Dave shrugged his shoulders, thinking, *Another elusive one. . . .*

"Frankly, I didn't really care all that much," he says. "I had more important issues to deal with, like being out of work and hopelessly in debt and experiencing slowly thinning hair!"

In 1988, Dave had left his job as a Calgary police officer in Alberta, Canada, investing his money in a new video production company. The promised business, however, did not materialize, leaving Dave in an extremely difficult financial position.

"Luckily," he says, "I was able to scrape enough work together to make payments on the loan and barely survive.

"One day I was driving home on the freeway in my newly acquired, downgraded vehicle—an almost completely rusted out, two hundred dollar 1979 Volkswagen—watching people drive by in their much newer, much larger car payments. I think there might have been a kid on a skateboard that passed me, too!"

Dave would like to say that in the midst of his troubles he could still praise God for His goodness and provision.

"In reality," he says, "I was whining and complaining, telling Him that I wasn't a big fan of what had happened over the past couple of years, and what was currently happening. I went on and on for quite some time about how bad things were—just so it was made unmistakably clear to Him. I suggested to God that I should go back into police work, perhaps in a different city. Vancouver? Toronto? Perhaps the coastal climate would be better."

At this point, Dave clearly heard God's voice in his spirit.

"He interrupted my one-way conversation and simply said 'The Israelites wanted to go back to Egypt, too.' Nine words. After all I had gone on about, that was it! Nine words, but they hit me like lightning. Could it be that *I* had been delivered? But to this? I wondered if there was a 'no questions asked' return policy.

"I continued home, closed myself in my room, and fell face-down on the floor for what turned out to be seven hours, with the presence of God surrounding me. When it was over, two things were unmistakably clear. I knew that God was with me, cared immeasurably for me, and would carry me through *it all*—whatever 'it' was.

"The second unmistakably clear thing was that the carpet really, really needed cleaning!" Dave laughs. "I was single at the time. Vacuum cleaner? I'd heard about them. Interesting concept. . . ."

Despite the pivotal spiritual experience that had occurred that day, Dave found that it was still tough to be spiritual when nothing in life was going as he'd hoped. This was his state of mind on the day "Awesome in This Place" came into being.

"One late winter morning [in 1991] with nothing to do, I sat at the piano with the sun streaming through the window," he says. "I played for a while with no particular direction, then accidentally played the first chord of what would be the finished song. What happened next was rather interesting, indeed. It was like a very clear connection to heaven opened, and the song spilled out, line-by-line in sequential order, until it was finished in about five minutes. Quite frankly, it was a challenge to keep up. I played it a few times until I had learned it, then it began to sink into my heart and minister to me."

> *You are awesome in this place, mighty God.*
> *You are awesome in this place, Abba Father.*
> *You are worthy of all praise,*
> *To You our lives we raise.*
> *You are awesome in this place, mighty God.*

"The presence of God invaded the room and surrounded me for some time. It was so beautiful, thick, and powerful; the only thing I could do was lift my hands and cry. I didn't think God would want to visit Canada in the winter, but apparently He does care about us! I don't know how many times I played the song that day, but it ministered so deeply to me in the midst of my circumstances."

After that, Dave had a new perspective, although financially things were getting worse.

He shared the song at his local church and was surprised at the impact it had on the congregation. Then in October of 1991, Dave met worship leader Kent Henry at a worship conference in Calgary. Dave asked if Kent would be willing to listen to his song, so Kent asked him to put it on tape.

"I tracked down the sound man near the end of the lunch break to see if we could do a quick version," says Dave. "Just me, a keyboard, and microphone, with nobody in the auditorium so I wouldn't get blamed for emptying out the conference!

"I started playing, and the musicians began filtering back in, coming up to the stage, to the point where we had a full band. Kent came in and sat at the piano, and was speaking with someone. I thought we had enough on tape, and as I was winding it down, he turned and said 'Play it again.' Fortunately, my name is not Sam! So off we went again. Kent started playing along after he had finished his conversation, and as I was ending again, he said 'Play it again.' I thought 'It's not my session! I came to hear you, Kent!' The auditorium was almost full by that point, people were singing, and there was a sweet presence of the Lord. I wondered, 'Are you going to let me off this stage?' We did a few more laps around heaven with the song, then Kent had his tape, and his session back."

After the session, Kent talked to Dave about sending the song to Integrity Music. Dave did exactly that, then forgot all about it.

Worship leaders who had attended the conference began asking for the music. A publisher also inquired about the song. It seemed to be the answer to Dave's financial woes. But repeatedly, he felt the Lord saying "No" to his requests to publish the song.

"Eventually, being a master of the obvious, I began to sense that God might know something I didn't," says Dave. "I decided it might be okay to trust Him; we ended the conversation."

By this time, Dave was working again in video production. In July of 1992, his last scheduled video project was winding down, and he wondered once again where his next loan payment, rent, and meal would come from. Then he was offered a job in Edmonton, farther north.

Within a few months, Dave received a letter from Integrity Music in response to his submission, telling him they would not be able to use "Awesome in This Place." Then, just two days later, he received a call from the company telling him that they were doing another project with Kent Henry and asking if Dave would like to sign his song.

"I thought this was rather odd considering the letter two days prior. Perhaps God was at work and really was for me," says Dave.

"The contract arrived a couple of days later. I asked God about it; he said 'Yes.' One word . . . and no argument from me. I was completely shocked when 'Awesome' was released as the first song on Integrity's *The Secret Place* in early 1993, and then was the title track on Kent's own release, *Awesome in This Place*, in April 1993."

Since then, an amazed Dave has watched the song go around the world. The song was nominated for a Dove award in 1997 and has touched an untold number of lives.

"I'm grateful that I had nothing to do on that winter's day in 1991 in the midst of a great sea of uncertainty and turmoil. I can look back now and see the hand of God at work in my life when I couldn't see it then. He truly was—and is—awesome in this place: my heart.

"I sometimes wonder if that song may have been popular in heaven," Dave muses. "Perhaps it was declining on the charts, and they wanted to try it out in a new market. You know how things go after thousands of years. . . ."

Dave remains thankful for the work God did in his life through "Awesome in This Place."

"At times I find it difficult to believe God gave me such a gift in that song. I remember the day with incredible clarity, even though it was ten years ago. I still have the original piece of paper it was written on.

"Through those very difficult years to the present, I've seen that being obedient to God concerning the stewardship of the song and all other numerous and ongoing issues of life has had its rewards. I'm now free of the once debilitating debt, I'm married, and have gained a basic working knowledge of vacuum cleaners!"

In the end, Dave has just one regret, which he adds with a wry smile.

"Being obedient has, unfortunately, not stopped my hair from thinning. But that's okay. I wear a hat in the winter."

"Awesome in This Place" by Dave Billington, © 1992, Integrity's Hosanna! Music/ ASCAP, c/o Integrity Media, Inc., 1000 Cody Road, Mobile, AL 36695.

5
_____

BE YE GLAD

MICHAEL KELLY BLANCHARD

"A song that I think is going to be a winner lays there like an egg. Another song I think is going to be problematic becomes the one everyone talks about."

Michael Kelly Blanchard seems to have been destined to write songs for the church.

Raised in a loving Catholic home where God was worshiped wholeheartedly, Michael considers the arts among God's greatest blessings.

Michael's mother was an English teacher who specialized in Shakespeare; his father was "a fiddler *extraordinaire.*" This creative environment set the stage for a love of God, a love of music, and a love of words, which have remained with Michael throughout his life.

"My upbringing was not what you'd call conservative evangelical," Michael says. "It was more liberal, from the standpoint that involvement in the arts was a very strong center. But in my late teens and early twenties, my faith and belief intensified, and that brought my work and interest into the more evangelical part of Christendom."

Although Michael has enjoyed a great deal of success in the Christian music industry, the concept would have struck him as strange when he was a boy.

"The term 'Christian music' would have never entered my home at all. It was all music and we were Christians who were singing it. The term 'Christian' was emphasized more as a noun than as an adjective. It was all good. In other words, God gives good gifts, so as a person—as a believer—you could touch anything you knew and bring redemption to it, as long as it was in alignment with God's will."

Michael has been writing songs since he was twelve years old. Fueled by his family background, he grew both as a believer and as a musician. In time, Michael began performing in local clubs and coffeehouses. He later studied composition at Berklee College of Music and went on to record numerous albums, as well as to write two music dramas, one cantata, several short stories, and two novels.

In 1979, Michael was in his early thirties and living with his wife Greta in Connecticut when they realized that one more song was needed for his upcoming album, *Love Lives On*. Michael wanted to write a song that would showcase Greta's rich alto voice as well as be a defining anthem for the project. At the time, his mind was filled with images of two different current events.

"The media on all fronts was full of the Iranian hostage crisis," he says. "So a good deal of the visual pictures in the piece have to do with prisoners and prison itself. What was also happening at that time—and getting nowhere near the press—was the genocide in Cambodia and the horrors being experienced by the boat people. These wrenching images were filling my soul."

Throughout this period, Michael was also spending time in the Psalms. "I was partial then to the *New English Bible*, and I still like it very much today; it strikes a balance between poetry and clarity that I find few translations do. Somewhere in there was a reference to 'be ye glad.' I copped it, and the song wrote itself very quickly. It was almost to prove that the Senior Partner in the deal had stepped into the song to make sure it came out right! The Senior Partner, being the Creator of all, knew He couldn't give me too much time or I'd start messing it up. So it came out real fast. I can't take much credit, except for being His conduit."

The song was written probably within an hour, the melody, first verse, and last verse.

"My wife, who sings with me on all the albums, immediately harmonized it. My folks came over sometime that evening and we played it for them because we were enjoying it so much. They flipped! They said, 'That's a winner!'"

Other confirmation quickly followed after Michael sent a copy of the song to Noel Paul Stookey—solo recording artist, songwriter, and member of the group Peter, Paul, and Mary.

"I sent 'Be Ye Glad' on a rough tape to Noel because he had recorded a song of mine the year before, and I wanted him to hear this one. He wrote back saying that he absolutely loved it, but that I should write another verse because it really was a hymn, he felt, and in that capacity it was just a little bit short. I looked at it and said, 'He's right.' The middle verse came right after that, quickly like the other two. At that point, I sent it back to him and he had already worked it up for his road band, called 'Bodyworks.' Ironically, they never used the lines he advised me to write. The new verse I included, of course, on our album that we recorded in 1980 called *Love Lives On*. Knowing that Noel loved that tune so much, we decided to record it in his studio up in Maine. It was just a blessed time.

"Shortly thereafter, I was out in Oregon at a youth workers convention and was on the same stage with the group Glad. We clearly connected. We had a very simpatico view of the arts. They came to town six months later and I gave them *Love Lives On*. They called me up later and said that they were going to do 'Be Ye Glad.' They've used it twice now, on an album called *Captured in Time* and on their first *a cappella* album."

When asked why he thinks people have responded so strongly to the song, Michael sounds genuinely puzzled.

"I can't read that. A song that I think is going to be a winner lays there like an egg. Another song I think is going to be problematic becomes the one everyone talks about. I know what I like and I think I know what people like . . . and again and again I've been absolutely wrong.

"I love this quote from Fred Rogers. He said, 'From my lips and to their ears is the land of the Holy Spirit.' In other words, between my mouth and others' ears the Holy Spirit does what He wants."

Though the song talks about being glad, it also touches upon some of the more difficult aspects of the human condition.

From the dungeon a rumor is stirring,
You have heard it again and again.
But this time the cell keys are turning
And outside there are faces of friends.
And though your body lay weary from wasting,
And your eyes show the sorrow they've had,
Oh the love that your heart is now tasting
Has opened the gates, be ye glad. . . .
There is no disease or no struggle
That can pull you from God, be ye glad. . . .

The blending of the two concepts, Michael says, is crucial.

"In both the Old and New Testaments, the word 'mercy' comes up a lot. Even the term 'grace' is a little too academic for a lot of us, but 'mercy' is a bullet right to the heart.

"We've all had this happen, where we've heard the sermon of the unconditional love of God, followed by twenty-nine conditions to that unconditional love. But the nature of mercy is that there are no conditions. He is by nature merciful, but a lot of people feel like they don't make the cut. They're in the pews, they're out in the streets, they're all over the place, and one of the things they just can't believe is that God's mercy would include them.

"No one is immune from brokenness," Michael observes, "but there is a larger, forgiving love that transcends our present state.

"And that is what the 'gladness' is about."

Oh, be ye glad, Oh, be ye glad.
Every debt that you ever had
Has been paid up in full by the grace of the Lord.
Be ye glad, be ye glad, be ye glad.

6

CELEBRATE JESUS

GARY OLIVER

"If you'll give me thirty minutes," Gary told her, "I'll write you a song."

When Gary Oliver took the job as music director he was still a child himself.

That perhaps explains why, from his earliest days at Truth Church (originally the First Pentecostal Church of Fort Worth), Gary has felt an affinity for children. Having grown up singing in church, young Gary felt natural stepping into a music ministry position.

"I've been around the music part of ministry and played piano and organ in church since I was about ten years old and sang in church the first time when I was two. They stood me on a little folding chair and put the mic all the way down so I could sing. I've sung ever since."

Gary started out as the associate music director at Truth Church when he was just thirteen. By the early 1980s, Gary was in his early twenties and serving as music director of the same church. One day, while preparing an Easter musical, the director of the children's department approached Gary with a compelling problem—one shared by churches around the world.

"She said to me, 'I think that all of the songs about Easter are a little frightening and morbid to the kids. Most Easter songs are slow, and they all talk about death and about Jesus dying on a cross. It's all kind of weepy. I would love to have something that would help the children understand that we can celebrate his death, burial, and resurrection.'"

As she spoke, Gary heard the words "Celebrate Jesus" in his head.

"If you'll give me thirty minutes," Gary told her, "I'll write you a song."

Gary, who had already written several praise and worship songs for the church, viewed the program from a child's perspective. "I thought, *What are we trying to get them to understand?* That we are celebrating Jesus' resurrection. It wasn't just that he died; it was that he died *and rose.* A lot of people die, but nobody else got up. I really wanted the children to understand that Easter celebrates Jesus and that the reason we celebrate Him is not just because He died but because He lives and He rose again.

"I sat down at the piano and sang the song the way I wrote it. I never fussed with the music. I never fussed with the lyrics. Literally, the whole A and B part of that song came in less than thirty minutes."

Later, Gary taught the song to the congregation's youngest children—from toddlers up to age eight—who sang it on Easter morning near the end of the church's Easter production.

"I remember it like it was yesterday," Gary says. "My eyes are watering thinking about it! The greatest joy of my life was seeing those kids clapping their hands and stomping their little feet, singing, 'Celebrate Jesus!' at the top of their lungs."

Gary says that the adults in the church "just went nuts" when the children started singing the song. He turned around to find that the 125-person adult choir had started spontaneously singing along with the kids.

"I looked out over our audience and people were in the aisles, jumping and dancing and praising God, their hands up and glorifying God while we sang that song. It was a sweet, innocent moment. It was very childlike worship. There was no pretense. It wasn't a religious, learned part of worship. People really were liberated in their spirit because, if you think about it, when you come to Jesus, you have to come to Him as a child."

Soon, the entire twelve-hundred-plus member congregation was singing along.

"The amazing thing was, that song was supposed to have been

just a little song at the end of the play. The kids had one scene left; I think it was the Ascension. We never finished the play. We sang that song for forty-five minutes the first time I ever sang it. It was really amazing. We stopped the song and the place would rejoice, and it was just a roar of praise. The next thing you know, we were right back into it and everybody was weeping."

When that happened, Gary realized that there was something truly amazing about his little song. Soon, through no effort on his part, the song would be published—although not under Gary's name, at first.

"It got published: 'Author unknown,'" he says. "The song was recorded by Integrity Music and they didn't know who wrote it. They chased me down, and I think the song had been out probably six or eight months before they ever found me."

It's still a mystery to Gary how the song found its way to the publisher, although he suspects it may have been passed on by one of the itinerant evangelists or ministers who heard it sung at Truth Church. "I know that that's partly how it got out. I really don't know how Integrity heard it.

"It was really, really interesting. That song went everywhere. It exploded. Even before it was recorded, it went everywhere and then, of course, with Integrity behind the song, it literally has gone all over the world. I've walked into churches in Stockholm and heard them sing it. I've walked into churches in Indonesia and heard them sing it. Every time, it makes me weep, and it makes me rejoice in the Lord to think that He would use this little East Texas country-boy to write a song that would literally go all over the world. I'm very, very thankful."

Although the song today is a popular favorite of both adults and children, Gary remains committed to the idea of putting spiritual truth into the language of the very young.

"My whole premise for writing this song was to help children understand. If you were to come and sit in my church you'd understand a little more why that means so much to me. The parishioners at our church tell me, 'The thing we love is your depth of the understanding of the Word of God, but you break it down so that a five year old can understand it.' That's very important to me because sometimes we just shoot over our children's heads. Everything we do is for us when, really, everything we do should be for them.

"I'm trying to set my children in motion so that they don't have the same battles and the same struggles that I did. They can have a deep understanding of the Word of God, and understand His love for them and His mercy and grace toward them. So everything that we do is for the children, it's for our youth. It's for those coming after us, because when we leave, what are we going to leave behind?"

This truth is particularly important to Gary since the death of his teenage son. His middle child was killed instantly after an unlicensed peer drove the car in which he was riding into a tree.

"We can't change anything that's already gone. That's why Jesus said, 'Let the dead bury the dead,' which makes more sense to me today, after burying a seventeen-year-old son, than ever before in my life. This song has become even more important to me in the last couple of years."

Despite their heartbreaking loss, Gary and his family remain committed to trusting in God—and to celebrating Jesus in the midst of their circumstances.

"Eighty or 85 percent of marriages that go through the loss of a child end up in divorce. What could have been a devastating blow to our marriage has actually turned into a very painful beauty mark in our marriage. It's made my wife and me very strong—strong in the Lord and strong with our family—and very committed to what we feel that God has called us to.

"It's been very, very painful, but the focus has to be that God is always in control. In everything that the Enemy might mean for evil—that comes to destroy your life, or to destroy your faith in God, or destroy your confidence—if you will not focus on the negative side of it, but focus on the positive effects of it, you can always see the hand of God."

Story approved by Gary Oliver.

7

Change My Heart, Oh God

Eddie Espinosa

"I never, ever expected or wanted anybody else to hear that song, because it was . . . my confession to God."

Eddie Espinosa wanted . . . needed . . . more of God in his life.

He knew, though, that some things in his life were preventing that from happening.

In 1982, twenty-eight-year-old Eddie had been a Christian for more than a decade. His life was rich with blessings: He was married with two children—a three-and-a-half-year-old daughter and ten-month-old son. He worked as a resource teacher at an elementary school and was leading worship at the rapidly growing, two-year-old Vineyard Christian Fellowship in Anaheim, California.

Still, he wanted to be closer to God.

"I had a sincere, heartfelt hunger," he recalls. "Yet there were things in the way—complacency and dissatisfaction. I wanted to get closer to the Lord, but there were things in my life, attitudes, that weren't pleasing to God."

One day, Eddie's heart cry spilled out as he was driving his Datsun 280Z to work.

"I was driving down the street and I realized that in my heart I had attitudes and appetites that Paul calls 'the flesh.' I said aloud, 'God, do something, change my appetites, change my desires. That's the only way I'm going to be free, so, God, I need you to change my heart.'"

As these thoughts and feelings absorbed him, Eddie found himself slipping into a time of spontaneous worship.

"Often, I'll have a worship time with the Lord, singing songs that I know. In this case, I began singing a song that I *didn't* know, but that was coming straight from my heart. It was almost like I was taking dictation," he says. "It just came. It was a heartfelt prayer.

"I've gotten a few like that. I really remember it when it happens, because it's like, 'Man, *this* is what I want to say to God. This is where I'm at right now.' At the same time, it comes so freely, I feel as if somebody else is behind the whole thing.

"It just blew me away," Eddie says of his experience in the car that morning. "I had a real tearful moment, almost like an altar call."

Two decades later, Eddie still sounds surprised by the process by which the song came.

"I almost can't take credit for the song. But at the same time, I know that's exactly where I was at. The crazy thing is, I never, ever expected or wanted anybody else to hear that song, because it was my Psalm 51—my confession to God. It's like that old song, 'Spirit of the Living God, fall afresh on me. Melt me, mold me, fill me, use me.' It just came: 'Change my heart, Oh God, make it ever true.'"

Working around the car's stick shift, Eddie grabbed a scrap of yellow paper and wrote down the lyrics as they came to him.

Change my heart, oh God,
Make it ever true.
Change my heart, oh God,
May I be like You.
You are the potter,
I am the clay,
Mold me and make me,
This is what I pray.

Originally, the words "Make it ever true" came out "Make it ever new." Eddie later changed the phrasing. "That was the only thing that I toyed with in the lyrics of the song," he says. "It came almost like taking dictation, but I knew that it was a cry from within me: 'My God, I just need you to change my heart. I don't want to be lukewarm anymore. I don't want to be complacent anymore. I don't want to play at this anymore.'"

Although Eddie had no intention of sharing this very personal song, God had other plans.

"My wife and I were leading a home group, and in that group were a few single people and about three or four couples. We made it a point once a month to have communion as a home group. One night we were having communion, and I was singing a couple of communion-type songs. Then I began singing 'Change My Heart, Oh God' to the group as part of worship. I repeated it a few times and they sang it. I didn't announce to them, 'Hey, I've written this song. Tell me what you think.' I just used it."

Eddie shared the song perhaps a month or so after he'd written it: "After I was able to sing it and get through it, if you know what I mean," Eddie says. "I didn't intend to share it; it seemed appropriate at the time."

From that home group, the song made its way to Eddie's pastor, Vineyard leader John Wimber.

"Somebody said to John, 'Hey, Eddie's written this song.' So he came up to me on Sunday—because I was playing guitar on the worship team at the time—and said, 'Eddie, I hear you've written a song. Would you play it for me?' So, I played it.

"He said, 'You've got to share that with the body.'"

"And I said, 'Today?'"

John's response was immediate. "Today."

Two weeks later, Eddie learned that a non-Vineyard church in San Diego had picked up the song. Without any effort on his part, it had begun to spread throughout the greater church. In subsequent months, the Anaheim Vineyard recorded *He's Worthy of Our Praise*, an album that included Eddie's song, as well as songs written by other members of the church. The song's popularity only grew.

That the song is so widely recognized, however, is not what brings Eddie the most satisfaction.

"I'm amazed at how God has used it," he says. "I'm humbled by it. It's an incredible blessing for me." Eddie reports that the greatest blessing he received from the song came to him while he was leading worship at a conference in England.

"This guy came up to me—he was about my age, maybe a little older—and said, 'Are you Eddie Espinosa?' And I said, 'Yes.' And he said, 'Did you write, "Change My Heart, Oh God"?' And I said, 'Yes.' And he put his arms around me and started crying. Before I knew it, I was weeping and I didn't know what it was all about."

The man explained to Eddie that some time before, his wife had been trying to get him to go to church, but he refused. She persisted, and one day he agreed to go, just to appease her. When the worship songs appeared on the overhead screen, he sang along with the congregation. And when "Change My Heart, Oh God" came up, he sang that, too.

"Eddie," he later reported to the songwriter, "I got saved singing your song, because I prayed it as I sang it."

"I was blown away by that," Eddie says. "More than anything—more than hearing bunches of people singing it, or hearing it on the radio, or backed up by an orchestra, or even at Promise Keepers—that was the one thing: to know that this one brother came into the kingdom singing that song. I thought, 'Man, if it's never sung again that's enough for me.' It made my lifetime worthwhile.

"And I didn't get his name, can you believe that? It was a, 'Who was that masked man?' kind of thing!"

When asked why he thinks the song has been so popular, Eddie doesn't hesitate.

"Three things: It's simple, it's honest, and it says what people want to say to God but maybe don't have the words to say. We all eventually come to a point in our lives where we say, 'God, change my heart.' I pray that I never lose that as a heart-life theme.

"I pray that I never get tired of singing that song to the Lord only."

8

Come into the Holy of Holies

JOHN SELLERS

"I cringe when I hear the words 'God gave me this song.'"

As a boy, John Sellers's lifestyle was unique. So was his musical training. Author of the stirring praise and worship song "Come into the Holy of Holies," John got his musical training in the army. The Salvation Army.

In fact, his parents were both officers in the organization. Like families attached to a secular military unit, members of the Salvation Army are obliged to move every few years when they are transferred.

In the 1960s, says John, the Salvation Army trained its children to play music when they were still young. "Just as soon as you could breathe and sit up, you had a horn in your mouth," he claims.

Such training would ultimately have a profound impact on the songwriter.

"A lot of the structure in my writing is influenced by the Salvation Army band arrangements," he reflects. "I was trained in four-parts, because that's the basic setting in a brass band. The trumpet section—you know, first and second trumpets—were called cornets."

He quickly became an outstanding horn player. By the time he reached the seventh grade, he was far ahead of his peers in the junior high band. Popular music was changing, however, and when the Beatles came along, John attempted to make the switch to piano.

"My mom had tried to make me take lessons before I was ten years old," he says, "but I just wouldn't do it. I thought it was sissy stuff."

After hearing Paul McCartney play, however, John regretted his lack of foresight. At just that time, the church's piano player quit, opening up new opportunities for him to play within the church. The only song John could pound out on the piano, however, was "Let It Be."

Undaunted, the pastor laid hands on the nineteen-year-old and prayed over him. The following Sunday, John started playing the piano—and he's never stopped.

"That was definitely a gift," he explains. "I believe that God gave me the piano for that purpose [worship], because I didn't play it before."

The teenager continued to serve in his home congregation. In time, however, John felt himself called out of the Salvation Army and into a new church experience.

Ready to try something new, he moved to Paducah, Kentucky, where he became involved with a group of young believers. His experience there was transforming.

"For the first time in my life I was exposed to a type of outward praise and worship," John says. "I mean, we clap in the Salvation Army, and we thought *that* was radical! It was very structured: In the Salvation Army we clapped on the chorus of the song, but only on Sunday night.

"Anyway, I walked into the new church and these people . . . their hands were in the air. The song ends, and everybody's shouting at the top of their lungs. I said, 'Good *night*, what is *this?*' I was very uncomfortable at first."

But John soon became more at ease with the format. He continued to attend the gatherings, which featured concerts by such artists as Keith Green, Don Francisco, and Terry Talbot.

Soon, John became inspired to create music for God. "I started saying, 'Hey, there's no reason why I can't write this stuff. God's got me here.'"

The community of believers discovered his musical talents, and John began filling in on the piano when Randy Rockwell's touring Praise Band came to town.

Before long, John was asked to start leading worship at the church. One thing led to another and, because John did not enjoy much of the praise and worship music that was available, he started writing his own. One of the first two songs he composed was the now classic "Come into the Holy of Holies," which quickly became a favorite of the body.

The song was born out of John's experience with a new type of teaching.

"The Salvation Army," he explains, "teaches basic salvation and sanctification doctrine. I never got into any conceptual teaching; it was all very basic."

In his new environment, however, John found that his peers were engaging in discussions that were directly sparked by sermons.

One talk, in particular, caught his attention.

"This one guy talked about how he played football with God in his imagination. He talked about how much he loved his son, and he loved to play football with him. Then he would meditate, saying, 'God, why can't I have this experience with you?' So in his imagination, he'd run for a pass, and God would throw him the pass. The point was, there's a personal relationship [with God] that's beyond what you know in your head—a communion aspect."

John also began to study about the temple and its allegorical connection to praise and worship, including the concept of entering God's courts with praise.

"After hearing the story about how the priest went in only once a year with a rope tied to his leg to drag him out, a person just thinks about this fear-motivated place: the temple."

Writing "Come into the Holy of Holies," says John, was about "realizing that Jesus' ministry was the ripping of the veil, so that we actually could come into the holy of holies."

Years passed before John approached Buck Herring about engineering the project. Buck was enthusiastic about the idea and tapped Dan Collins to produce the song. Artists such as Annie Herring, Nellie Griesen, Matthew Ward, Jamie Owens, and Buddy Owens agreed to perform vocals. Buck further offered to call legendary Christian music executive Billy Ray Hearn on John's behalf. The song and its recording soon began a journey around the world.

A missionary told John that the song was being sung in a remote jungle in Africa. "There were natives in this village singing 'Come into the Holy of Holies' in their native tongue," he says, "and I thought, 'Good grief! Thank you, Lord. What's going on here?'"

He admits, "It's funny, the way songs come. I cringe when I hear the words 'God gave me this song.'" John has heard that line so much over the years, he says, "I used to joke, 'Yeah, because He didn't want it anymore.'"

But, says John, there truly was a time when "as fast as I could write 'em, I was writing them. All the songs in this period, the words and the music were coming simultaneously, and I'd have to stop and write that line and then go on and play the next line, stop and write that line. . . . That's how it was happening, with the whole process not taking more than three minutes."

Today, John works with a group of independent artists from all over the country whom he has organized into a worship band known as the Pray Heads. John continues to produce albums and video projects.

He's also just enjoying life.

"We get caught up in so many things," he warns. "The older I get the more I realize that every day is an absolute gift from God. I tell myself, 'You have a wonderful wife, John. Just love her and enjoy your life to the max every day, every moment.'

"You know," he says thoughtfully, "you can't save the world. You may have a part in it, or you may be on the cutting edge, or you may have just a small part.

"But you have to take time to just enjoy this life that God has given you."

Story approved by John Sellers.

9

Come, Let Us Worship and Bow Down

DAVE DOHERTY

"All of a sudden everything hit me at once. I had to pull off to the side of the road. I bawled like a baby for about a half an hour."

At nineteen years old, Dave Doherty found himself back in high school again . . . and again . . . and again. . . .

But he wasn't a student.

He was an evangelist.

Inspired by Christian bands like Love Song, which came out of southern California in the 1960s, Dave and three of his friends had formed a Christian folk/rock band of their own: The Brethren. The name was a perfect fit, for the four friends were as close as brothers, even sharing living quarters.

"We were living together in a little house in Seattle," says Dave. "I think we paid a hundred and five dollars a month, because we had no income besides what we generated in the group, and that was just free-will offerings."

Beginning in 1970, the group ministered extensively, primarily to youth, performing most of their concerts at high schools, junior high schools, and colleges. Sponsored by local outreach groups like Young Life or Campus Crusade, the band would travel to an area to perform at one or two schools per day, throughout the week. At the end of the week, they would do a final concert at a neutral location, such as a grange hall. The band ministered to as many as seven hundred kids at a time, reaching out to them through music, testimonies, and a clear presentation of the gospel. After the concerts, band members would stay and counsel the kids, then help plug them into local youth groups and churches.

The band's success eventually led them to tour the East Coast, where they formed an immediate bond with the pastor of a church in New Jersey. Before the young men headed back to Seattle, the pastor took them aside and invited them to join his staff. After taking a month off to go home and regroup, The Brethren decided to step out in faith and make the move east.

In New Jersey, one band member worked at a halfway house in the city of Elizabeth, while Dave and the other two band members worked full-time with youth at the church. The four continued in this ministry for approximately a year and a half.

Then in 1974, three members of The Brethren moved on to other areas of ministry. Dave stayed on as the sole youth/assistant pastor of the congregation.

He remained at the church for one more year. There, he met his future wife, whom he married in 1975. But the strain of working without his former partners in ministry took a toll on Dave. He and his wife left the church approximately six months after their wedding.

"I'd gotten disillusioned," Dave said. "Having worked with those guys for so many years, I hadn't realized the impact it had. But all of a sudden I was there by myself." Dave also struggled, realizing that the church was no longer growing as it had when he first came on staff.

"I felt like I didn't fit there anymore. So I left and that's when I really hit the skids, spiritually. After being so intensely involved in ministry for so many years, all of a sudden I was doing nothing, as far as ministry goes. It was a huge adjustment I hadn't anticipated."

A time of struggle followed his departure from the ministry.

"During that time, I questioned a lot of things. I put a lot of blame on God, and on the people in the church, and on my pastor. My wife and I never really got plugged into a new church. So for about a year, we were really in the wilderness."

Still, the bills had to be paid. So to support his family, Dave went to work driving a delivery van. "I think I was making a hundred and twenty dollars a week. I'd been out of the job market for years, so I had no marketable skills."

The transition from full-time ministry continued to be difficult and painful. After a while, Dave turned to music to help him cope. He spent a lot of his reflective time with his guitar, writing songs and reading the Psalms. He also listened to a fair amount of radio.

"I always listened to the radio in the delivery van. A guy named Clinton White broadcast from way up in New Hampshire. He had a talk show on a Christian radio station a couple of hours a day. He was an amazing guy, and everything he said seemed to speak to me."

One day while he was listening to White, all of Dave's buried emotions pushed their way to the surface.

"I was driving down the Jersey Turnpike between all these big trucks, making a delivery, and all of a sudden everything hit me at once. I had to pull off to the side of the road. I bawled like a baby for about a half an hour. After that, I felt this peace and this cleansing. I felt like things were going to be okay.

"I was feeling a lot of stuff, but I was afraid to verbalize it. I'm not a touchy-feely person. With people like me, when the emotions come out, they come out all at once, unplanned. I think that experience on the Jersey Turnpike was the Lord's way of getting it all out where He could begin to deal with it. And He did, He really did."

The floodgates had opened and the healing had begun. Yet there was one more blessing on its way.

Two days later, while sitting in a little TV room that he had converted into a makeshift recording studio, Dave wrote the now-famous worship song, "Come, Let Us Worship and Bow Down," an experience made possible by the work God was doing in his broken spirit.

"The song came at the culmination of a lot of disappointment," he says today, "a combination of being confused and not knowing what to do, and being kind of desperate. The Lord brought me to that place where He said, 'If you just bow down and worship me, I'm going to guide you. I'll lead you. I'll take care of you. Don't worry about it.' I wrote the song probably in a day. I didn't labor over it. Like a lot of those songs, they flow out of what a person is going through at the time."

A couple of months later, Dave and his wife moved back to Seattle, where they started attending a small Calvary Chapel pastored by one of his former bandmates, Wayne Taylor. Dave shared his new song with Wayne. In the following months, Wayne, in turn, used it during a worship time at a conference held in California for pastors of Calvary Chapel congregations.

In attendance that day was renowned worship leader and songwriter Tommy Coomes. Tommy liked the new song so much, he made a point of tracking down its author.

Dave got a call from Maranatha! Music approximately one month later. It turned out that Maranatha! wanted to include the song on their *Praise 6* album. But first they had to confirm that Dave had truly written the song.

The gauntlet through which he was required to run was not exactly grueling. "The representative from Maranatha! asked me to sing the song back to her on the phone. So I did, and she said, 'Well, that's it. That's the song.'" The company then sent a formal contract for Dave to sign. "That was all the confirmation they needed. I don't think you'd see that happen now!" he marvels.

Decades later, he remains thankful for the lessons the song imparts.

"It taught me to just live in the moment with the Lord," he says, "and that if I stayed in the moment with Him, then I didn't have to be concerned about even tomorrow, let alone next month or next year. I learned that regardless of circumstance, living in the moment with Him—recognizing His presence, coming to that place of worship and acknowledging Him—brings me a lot of peace and a lot of confidence."

Dave also continues to be surprised by the song's success.

"It was never intended to get any kind of air play or any kind of popularity. It was just born out of my own experience, and I think it's wonderful that it blesses people. I don't take any credit for it. I wrote it, but the rest of it is the Lord's doing.

"God will take the smallest thing, and if He wants to increase it, He does."

Story approved by Dave Doherty.

10

Draw Me Close

KELLY CARPENTER

"I was crying as I wrote it. But I was also thinking, This sounds like a Barry Manilow song."

Kelly Carpenter's impact on the music world was different than he'd intended or dreamed.

Raised in a Lutheran church, Kelly ultimately became saved through a Young Life program at his high school. His conversion, however, was quickly followed by a time of spiritual floundering.

"I fell away from the Lord for almost five years," he says. "I was just being a stupid, rebellious teenager. I was pursuing a dream of making it in the music business, because I was 'a musician.' I had aspirations of becoming a recording star. I went off and did my own thing for a while—even after I had come to know the Lord personally."

But Kelly's rebellion was short-lived. In 1980, when he was just twenty-one, Kelly says, "The Lord grabbed me, and I rededicated my life to Him. I got involved again in music, this time with Christian music, and I transferred my dream of being a musician of note in the secular arena to being a musician/performer of note in the Christian arena. I didn't quite get it yet."

Kelly married two years later, and in 1984, he and his wife Merrilyn first visited a Vineyard fellowship. "We really enjoyed the preaching style," he says. "We enjoyed the laid-back feel of it. We enjoyed the music . . . after a while. At first, we thought, *Why do people spend forty-five minutes singing songs?* We didn't quite understand what was going on with this whole worship thing."

Eventually, however, the Carpenters served on the church's worship team: Merrilyn as a vocalist, Kelly as a keyboardist. That's when the Lord began to change their hearts.

"It wasn't until 1990 that I started to understand what worship was about," says Kelly, "to understand that the Lord had called me to take the musical gift that He'd given to me, that He had created me for the purpose of worship. I started to experience in my playing something that I'd never experienced before: That was the anointing of the Lord for worship through what I played and how I played it."

In the early nineties, Kelly began to write his own worship songs, which he shared with friend, mentor, and Vineyard worship leader, Andy Park ("The River is Here"). In 1992, Kelly's commitment to praise and worship led him to take a position of leadership at his Vineyard Christian Fellowship congregation in Kirkland, Washington, when the previous worship leader stepped down.

Around this time, Kelly received a prophecy that the Lord was going to give him a number of songs. In fact, in 1993 and 1994, he did write several successful praise and worship tunes, including "Send Your Rain," and "Arise, O Lord."

The pressure and responsibility of leading a music ministry took its toll, however, and in January of 1994, Kelly realized that he had to make some serious changes in his life.

"I came home one Sunday after church," he says, "and recognized that my relationship with the Lord was kind of on the skids, even though I was in ministry. I recognized that I had allowed my ministry to take first place in my life—to the detriment of my relationship with the Lord. I think it happens to many people in all aspects of ministry. They get so caught up in doing what they feel they're supposed to be doing, all the day-to-day stuff—sometimes it's easy to neglect their own personal walk with the Lord. That's what happened to me.

"I sat down at the piano and started doing this heart cry to the Lord. The key verse in that song was 'I lay it all down again.' For me, that signified, 'I'd throw away all this ministry stuff that I'm walking in, 'cause I'd rather have You call me a friend than be considered some great minister.' That's pretty much the crux of the song. That was the key: 'I lay it all down again, to hear you say that I'm your friend.' It was one of those songs that just poured out, probably in about thirty minutes or so. I did very little refining after it came.

"It came out of my heart, and I cried as I wrote the song, but I also consider it something that God dropped in my lap."

At the time, however, Kelly did not recognize the depth of the song's beauty.

"Like I said, I was crying as I wrote it. But I was also thinking, *This sounds like a Barry Manilow song*. So I played it for my wife, and she said, 'Oh, that's a great song.' So I figured, maybe it isn't so dorky." He laughs.

By this time, Kelly was in the practice of sending his new songs to Andy Park. Andy liked "Draw Me Close" so much that he decided to use it on his *The River Is Here* album. He even asked Kelly, who he'd tapped to play on the album, to lead out on the song during the live recording.

Since that time, "Draw Me Close" has become a standard at congregations around the world—a fact that Kelly acknowledges with humble amazement.

"I really don't know why," he admits. "Plenty of other songs out there are poignant, expressed maybe even through similar themes. I haven't put a finger on what's really going to hit it off with people and what isn't. I can't explain why the song has taken off the way it has. I certainly can't go back to, 'Well it's because I combined this line with that line.' I can't deconstruct it that way; it's a mystery to me.

"God just gave us a gift, and He happened to give it through me, which delights me to no end. The Lord plants those seeds in people's hearts, and they sprout up. Some go far, some don't. . . . It's just a gift from the Lord."

In the years since "Draw Me Close" was written, Kelly has faced numerous challenges in life—including a life-threatening bout with pneumonia—and challenges in his music career, including a difficult, extended period in which his songwriting dried up completely. Yet through it all, he has remained committed to worship, serving in congregations as both an associate pastor and a worship pastor—a responsibility he takes more seriously today than ever.

Citing 2 Chronicles 20:20, Kelly reflects on the role of worship leaders who were, centuries ago, sent out by Jehoshaphat at the head of his army.

"I always viewed that passage as meaning we worship leaders are the first to be picked off by the Enemy. I had almost a defeatist attitude about that: *Yeah, we know the Lord's gonna save us from the fire. But you better get your shields up, because the Enemy is coming after us 'cause we're worship leaders and people on the worship ministry.* And it's true. We're on the front line. But I'd never realized that the worship leaders are at the head of the army for a reason: We're on the offensive. We don't have to go out there in fear and trembling: 'Oh, the Enemy's gonna get us.' It's more like, 'We're leading the army.' There's a prophetic side to worship, a warfare side to worship. And we're on the offensive. We're going to expand the kingdom.

"It's weird how I never really quite understood that," he reflects. "To me, this is an incredible privilege, to be at the head of the army. The Lord calls those who are in worship to be at the head, and to take the offensive, and to expand the kingdom.

"It's an awesome, awesome thing."

Story approved by Kelly Carpenter.

11

Father, I Adore You

TERRYE COELHO STROM

"I do not take credit. I did not write it. I just got to be the vessel to give it to the world."

Many people want to be labeled as songwriters, although they are *not*. It's rare, however, to come across a skilled songwriter who claims to be anything *but*. In fact, "Father, I Adore You," written in the 1970s by a talented teenager, may be one of the most famous songs ever written by someone who refused the label *songwriter*.

"I'm not a songwriter," Terrye Coelho Strom—now married and a mother of four—states definitely. "I absolutely love music. It's part of who I am, totally. But I play by ear; I don't have any training. I would say that the Lord gave me a gift of writing words. That's what people tell me, at least. I've written a lot of poetry and stories and things like that, but I've never aspired to be a songwriter, *per se.*"

Despite her lack of training as a songwriter—perhaps even be-cause of it—God chose Terrye many years ago to be the one through whom a simple, lovely, and now classic praise song would come into the world.

At the time, Terrye was a new believer. Just nineteen years old, she had become a Christian one year prior, on April 17, 1971. She quickly became involved with the ministry of Calvary Chapel in Costa Mesa, home to such early Christian bands as Hosanna, The Way, and Love Song, as well as the Maranatha! Music ministry.

When Terrye started attending, the church was still meeting in a small chapel. Not long afterward, it began meeting in a massive tent.

"It was such a wonderful, informal setting," Terrye recalls. "Anyone who wanted to share a song or a word or a testimony could just go up and share. It was held seven nights a week, and I was always there, even though I lived up in Fullerton. I'd just make that hour drive every night."

During the summer of 1972, Terrye drove to Newport Beach with her sister Cathy for a day of fun. On the way home in Terrye's old, green Maverick with the black and white plaid seats, the two girls started singing together, as was their custom.

"We always sang doing the dishes or whatever, our whole life growing up," says Terrye.

During the car trip, she and Cathy sang various praise and worship songs they knew from their respective home churches. Then Terrye spontaneously started singing a new song.

"I say this was of the Lord because it wasn't someone sitting down and writing a song; it was simply worshiping in the Spirit. I just started singing the song in worship as we were driving home. We thought it was really neat because we were doing it in a two-part round, but we could hear that it could go in a three."

Terrye says that other songs have come to her over the years before and after "Father, I Adore You." But before she has a chance to write them down, most are quickly forgotten. "Father, I Adore You" was easily recalled by both girls.

"It was something you could remember. God was going to make sure it got sung or used in worship because sometimes songs just leave me after singing them around the house. I think, *Oh, I wish I could remember that song*, and I can't."

This time, she did.

"Shortly thereafter, I shared it at Calvary Chapel," says Terrye, "and they just loved it."

Ernie Rettino, a friend from Calvary Chapel who worked with Maranatha! as a writer and producer, offered to get the song copyrighted. Soon, the song debuted on the Maranatha's *Praise Album*. Right around the same time, another of Terrye's songs, "Any Man," also known as "Matthew 16:24," appeared on *The Kids' Praise Album* and since has been featured on several other recordings. In subsequent years, Terrye performed in another of the bands to come out of Calvary Chapel—the group called Lamb. But musically, she is best known for "Father, I Adore You."

> *Father, I adore you,*
> *Lay my life before you.*
> *How I love you.*

"The thing that blesses me the most is when I hear how it has blessed other people's lives, how it has enhanced their worship," she says. "If people mean those words as they're singing them, well, you can't get any better than that! If you lay your life before the Lord and you adore Him and He's the center of your life and you love Him, that's it. That's all He asks.

"The song has been a blessing to me, and I know it's blessed other people," she says. "But, like I say, I do not take credit. I did not write it. I just got to be the vessel to give it to the world. I'm thrilled at that."

12

FAVORITE SONG OF ALL

DAN DEAN

"I always told my wife, 'I'd love to write at least one song that will outlive me.' I don't know that this one will, but I hope it does."

To fully understand the inspiration for "Favorite Song of All," one first must know the musical background of its author, Dan Dean, of the singing group Phillips, Craig, and Dean.

"I was raised doing a lot of black gospel music," he remembers. "Loved it. I *still* love it."

In the 1980s, Dan had just started making his own journey into praise and worship. Although the movement had, by that time, been around for a number of years, Dan was just becoming familiar with it. "I was a little slow getting on board," he confesses.

At the time, he was trying to move into new musical territory—to break away from familiar ground—and was familiarizing himself with a number of various groups and styles. One night, Dan attended an all-night concert.

"This particular night was filled with totally different kinds of music," he recalls. "There was praise music, there were black gospel choirs, there were quartets, other gospel groups . . . there was a representation of a lot of different styles. They even had some rap music, and the thought crossed my mind, *I wonder if God has a preference when it comes to any of this?* 'Cause I knew *I* did," Dan laughs.

"That's how this song started. Because that night, I realized at some point that music style doesn't really matter to Him. What matters to Him is that these people—whatever background they come from, whatever great thing God has done for them—are singing from a heart that's been set free. And they're doing it in the way they know how to do it.

"That's how the idea for the song started. It's one of those songs that came quickly after the inspiration was born.

"A few weeks later, my wife and I were in Maine. We went up there to sing in somebody's wedding. And we took a little trip around some of the coastline. There's a beautiful national park up there. And I saw those waves crashing. I thought, *Man, this is unbelievable!* It was like music, and I thought, *It has to be music to the ears of God.*

"I started thinking about what must gladden the heart of God. The first part of the first verse dealt with everything that sounds like music: waves and wind and the raindrops. But that's not what He *loves* to hear. He loves to hear what He can't give to Himself, and that's praise and worship from a heart that gives it voluntarily. It's nothing that's forced; it's from created beings who have a choice whether to praise or not to praise. When we worship and praise, that's the thing He loves to hear more than anything else.

"That's how the song was born, and I wrote the song in one day, with the exception of just a few lines."

The song was written several years before the first Phillips, Craig, and Dean album in 1991. But when it came time to choose songs for the group's debut release, Dan felt less confident in the song.

"What's really funny," he says, "is that I did the song in two or three different churches [before the recording]. Maybe it was the arrangement, the way I was doing it, but I never got a very good response. So when we went in to record it on the first PCD album, I hesitated. Everybody else said, 'Yeah, let's record this.' And I felt like, 'Man, I don't know.' The song had a whole country vibe going before. Then our first producer, Paul Mills, put it in the AC [adult contemporary music] vein, and I think it lifted the song to another level."

Not surprisingly, considering Dan's musical roots, it is a gospel rendition of the song that touched his spirit the most.

"I'll never forget the first time that we sang the song with the Brooklyn Tabernacle Choir," he says. "We were there, singing at their church. When that choir starts singing . . . oh, man! We were out in front of them, and when we finished the song there were just waves of worship for probably five to eight minutes. It never quit. It was a pretty phenomenal experience. I hope that the choir director of heaven maybe puts that on the song list someday. I'd like to hear it when we get up there, with everybody gathered. But it's probably a little too much to ask!"

Although Dan has written numerous songs, "Favorite Song of All" was a different experience in many ways.

"It's one of the few songs that I've written totally by myself," he says. "I usually co-write. I don't trust myself musically most of the time. I'm mostly a lyricist. But that particular song . . . A lot of people tell me they were driving down the road the first time they heard it, and they had to pull over. It's really a gratifying feeling. I always told my wife, 'I'd love to write at least one song that will outlive me.' I don't know that this one will, but I hope it does."

In addition to his music career, Dan has served as both a music minister and pastor. His role in the church inspires him the most.

"There is no greater honor than to carry people on the vehicle of worship into the presence of God," he says. "It's an incredible honor. I *love* doing it. I love that God has given me that gift. Sometimes it gets tedious when it's Sunday after Sunday after Sunday," he confesses. "Sometimes I have to step back and say, 'God, what I'm doing is so critically important, let me be willing to make changes on the fly if I have to,' which is hard for a lot of us to do. We come in with our list of songs and the direction we think it needs to go. Then all of a sudden God shows up and wants us to go in another direction, so we have to be flexible. But, man, what an opportunity! I can't think of any higher calling than leading people into the presence of God.

"It's like 'Favorite Song of All' says: It's hard to picture that God can resist when somebody who's been changed by the blood of Jesus Christ voluntarily praises Him in music. I think it draws His attention like a magnet.

"Proverbs 27:21 says, 'As the refining pot for silver, and the furnace for gold; so is a man to his praise' [KJV]. Isn't that a great Scripture? It signifies that praise helps to purify our lives. As we begin to praise, as we enter into worship, God starts a work of purification and cleansing in our lives.

"Occasionally, on the way to church, my wife and I might have a little argument. There's no way I can enter into worship—and have it be heartfelt worship—without addressing whatever problems I had on the way to church. So we've got this little sign that we give to each other to say, 'You know what? I was wrong. Forgive me. I can't really enter into worship until I get this taken care of.' So I'll be on the platform sometimes and flash her that little sign, just to let her know. And that's the way it is. You can't praise and do it in the way you want to do it if there's something in your heart that's clogging up the flow. 'As the refining pot for silver and the furnace for gold; so is a man to his praise.'

"I love it!"

Story approved by Dan Dean's assistant, on his behalf.

13

I Exalt Thee

PETE SANCHEZ JR.

"I got forced into a corner, to offer something I wasn't prepared to . . ."

Pete Sanchez Jr., felt suddenly and unexpectedly called to examine his life.

In the mid-1970s, Pete seemed to have the ideal music minister's life. Newly married, Pete did not yet have children, but he was mindful of his role as husband and his future role as father.

At twenty-six years old, he had come out of a three-year stint as a music director and youth director in a local church where he had a highly successful ministry. More recently, while living in Houston, Texas, he had begun ministering with the local music group One Song, a role that called for him to travel full time.

"I traveled and enjoyed that, but I came to a crossroads in my life. I felt like the Lord asked me to step away from the group. I needed to know what a good dad would be and what it would take to be a good husband. I came from a divorced family and knew I needed to do some work in my life. So I made a commitment that if I never sang again, if I never did the public thing again, at least I could face the Lord saying that I was a good husband, I was a good father."

Pete explains that he felt the Lord say to him, "If you will invest, if you will lay down your music ministry, there are better days ahead of you." Spurred on by this promise, Pete withdrew from One Song and, for a season, from public ministry. Initially, he made his living through freelance music work and later taught in a Christian school.

"For the next few weeks and months, I spent a lot of time in Psalms," he says. It was not the first time Pete had immersed himself in Scripture. "This time, though, it wasn't for any kind of public ministry," he says. "It was for personal growth. As part of that, I made a decision that I would like to write, at some point, a song from every psalm in the Bible."

As part of his personal discipline, Pete went to the Scriptures each day and spent time in the Psalms. Starting with Psalm 1, he sang whatever came up in his heart.

"As I worked my way through the Psalms," he says, "I came to this little, obscure verse in Psalm 97:9 which says, 'For thou, LORD, art high above all the earth: thou art exalted far above all gods.' [KJV]. For some reason or another, it jumped out at me. It caught my attention, kind of lodged in my heart.

"So—again, as part of my personal devotion, with nobody else around—I went to the piano and sang the first part of a song. And that's all I got. For months, every time I'd go to the Psalms, and every time I'd get to that place, I'd sing that little melody that I got from that one verse. I sensed that there needed to be more, but it would never come. I didn't press it, and I went on to other things. But, sure enough, every time I got into a time of personal devotion, that song would come up."

Then, in April of 1976—more than half a year after the first part of the song came to him—Pete got the break he'd been looking for.

"My wife was running a little bit late for church on Sunday," he says. "So, as was my habit, I went to the keyboard and started singing this song all over again." When Pete got to the end of the verse, something extraordinary happened.

"The only way I can explain it is that, in a moment, it seemed like I stepped into another place." The chorus immediately began rolling off Pete's tongue: "I Exalt Thee."

"It was a divine moment, a divine encounter," says Pete. "I physically sensed the presence of the Lord in the room and all around me as I sang that song. I had one of those really, really special moments. I thought, *Well, this is great! I've finished this song and I feel like I've offered something that will please the Lord.* I left it there and we went on to church."

A few weeks later, Pete was invited to attend a songwriter's conference in Goshen, Mississippi. At the gathering, each songwriter in attendance was asked to offer three of his or her best songs.

"These were all pretty good songwriters from all over the country. We were sequestered away in a little hotel, and I was the last one on the program," says Pete. "I sang the first two songs that were like 'Top 40' songs: well arranged, with good hooks. My best stuff. Everybody liked them and clapped politely. Then they asked me, 'Do you have anything else?'"

All Pete had left was his little song from Psalm 97:9: "I Exalt Thee." Although he considered it a very simple song—certainly not fitting for a songwriter's retreat—he began to sing.

"When I got to the chorus, a lightning bolt seemed to go through the room. Everybody shot to their feet, threw their hands in the air, and started singing at the top of their voices as though they knew the song. I was watching this phenomenon, watched all these people encountering God in a deep and personal way.

"I looked at this and thought, *You have it wrong. It was the first two songs that this was supposed to happen on, not this simple little song.* I didn't understand their excitement over the song because musically, it is so simple. Theologically, it's a simple statement. But for some reason it seemed to capture the heart of God and the desire for those people to worship.

"I left that conference and the next thing I know, the song left that little bitty hotel room and went all over the world. I never shopped it anywhere, never did anything with it. It just got all over the world fast, within a few years. It was never, ever my intention to sing that song outside of my apartment. It was just a simple offering."

After the songwriter's retreat, Pete realized that something bigger than him was at work. He quickly recognized the hand of the Lord.

"I was investing my life, and it was as though God said, 'Here, I'm giving you something back. You may think you're not doing music ministry anymore, but here's a treasure in a field.' God had an agenda and He chose to ambush me, give me a break: 'Here is a song. I want you to be a good steward of this.' I didn't go looking for anything to happen. I just feel grateful that it happened.

"That song came out of my hunger to be in the Scriptures and write something just for the Lord. I never planned to go public with it. I got forced into a corner, to offer something I wasn't prepared to do, and God took that moment to launch the song all over the world.

"Since then, every major publisher has used it, and I have files from every country in the world where people are singing it. I've been with all kinds of worshipers, all over the country, young and old, and they always tell me the same thing: If they are in a time of worship and things are down, and they can't get the people up, all they have to do is pull out 'I Exalt Thee' and people will get back into a place where they can be led into worship.

"It's been a phenomenal ride. I figure it's got just so much shelf life. About the time I think the song is over, and I'm grateful for what God's done with it, then comes the next new move of God around the country. Somebody will pick it up and start using it and it will ride a whole new crest again. I call it 'the Forrest Gump feather effect.' Just about the time it hits the ground, it catches another breath of wind and rides the next crest."

Although Pete is a skilled and highly trained songwriter, he hesitates to take much credit for the song.

"I'm a classically trained musician, so I know how to write songs. But I have a fear of the Lord when I talk about 'I Exalt Thee'—not to take credit for it. It's a gift that was given to me and I treat it that way."

After departing from One Song in the early 1980s, Pete did go back into full-time ministry. But he's still grateful for the time he spent away, which allowed him to invest more time in his new family—and to write "I Exalt Thee."

"I've walked into congregations of thousands and watched them sing this song and watched them literally go into the place where I felt I was that day on the piano. They get into a place of exalting the Lord, and the Lord dwells in the praises of His people. I've seen lives changed, and I'm always humbled by it because this song was totally a gift. The response to it wasn't anything I went looking for.

"I'm as amazed as anybody else, and I'm still amazed after all these years."

Story approved by Pete Sanchez Jr.

14

I Sing Praises to Your Name

TERRY MACALMON

"God walked over to the music library of heaven and went to the I's"

Somebody didn't want Terry MacAlmon to sing his song.

As talented worship pastor, Terry had just written what would become one of the most widely sung praise and worship songs of all time. But the song very nearly slipped into obscurity instead. And the story of what appeared to be a moment of personal reluctance provides a telling glimpse into the tactics of spiritual warfare, illustrating how the Enemy attempts to silence, weaken, and incapacitate God's people.

The year was 1986. Terry and his wife Greta had three sons, ranging from newborn to five years old. The MacAlmon family had recently moved to Loveland, Colorado, where Terry had accepted the role of worship pastor at a large charismatic church.

"The church was growing very, very quickly," says Terry. "We added something like one hundred people a month for, I'd say, a year and a half."

Among the church's blessings were its popular evening services. Each Sunday night before the service began, the pastoral and leadership staff gathered in the church's prayer room.

"We would all gather in the same room but each do our own thing for maybe thirty minutes before service," he says. "Then we'd come together with our different groups. All the worship team prayed together before we went out. But we'd spend the first several minutes on our own—which is when God walked over to the music library of heaven and went to the I's." He laughs. Terry clearly remembers one Sunday night in particular.

"I was worshiping Him quietly to myself, and I started to sing the first two or three lines of that song ["I Sing Praises to Your Name"]. I realized I was singing something I hadn't sung before, so I took the offering envelope, which is always in the front of my Bible, and jotted it down.

Typically, I'll get a half or three-quarters of a song right away and then I'll wait on the last part of it to come together." In this case, however, Terry says, "The whole song came before I left the prayer room."

Terry still carried the song lyrics when he went out to lead the congregation in worship that night. At that time, the congregation had grown to approximately two thousand people, and nearly half were in attendance at the evening service.

"The first part of our praise and worship session would be energetic, up-tempo. Then we'd transition to a slower time of worship. That night, at the end of that up-tempo time I felt like God said, 'Pull the song out of your Bible and sing it.' I hadn't played it yet or sung it for anyone." Neither had Terry planned to do so just yet.

"I had just jotted down words and a few notes and tried to give myself enough of a heads up, so whenever I took it out again I'd remember what I'd written. There are a few things I have to write down—such as tempos or rhythms or time—so I can regroup."

Terry didn't feel comfortable with the idea of playing the song without being able to first practice or fine-tune it.

"Whenever I do something on the spur of the moment, I'm always a little bit anxious. I remember sitting there at the piano—I led the service from there—and the Enemy said, 'Don't bother singing that song. It's not worth it. It's too simple. It's just a little ditty God gave you. It was for your own private time, so don't sing it.'"

Terry felt himself in a moment of crisis.

"I didn't do anything for the next fifteen seconds. But it seemed like fifteen minutes with a thousand people waiting for the next thing to happen, and I'm in charge and doing nothing but staring at the keyboard.

"And this battle was going on at warp speed in my heart: 'Sing it.' 'Don't sing it.' 'Sing it.' 'Don't sing it.' Probably, had I not sung it, I would have thrown it away. But I sang it.

"I said, 'I want to share a little chorus that God gave to me just before the service tonight.' It's such a simple song that it takes about fifteen seconds to learn. The people picked it up right away—even though we didn't have any overhead projection for it—and we sang it many times that night. A little rhythm section sat right behind me. The bass player came up to me after the service and said, 'Pastor Terry, when you were singing that song to me, the Lord showed me it being sung in nations all over the earth.'"

Terry says his immediate response was one of incredulity.

"I thought, *Oh, brother, this guy has flipped. It's just a simple little thing. How would it ever be sung any place but our sanctuary?* I thanked him cordially for his kind remark and, being the great man of faith that I am, I rolled my eyes as I walked away."

That man of faith, however, would eventually become convinced.

A year and a half after that service, Integrity Music was planning to record the worship album *Enter His Gates* at Terry's church. Terry submitted "I Sing Praises to Your Name" for consideration for the project.

Integrity evaluated the song based on their in-house rating system. "It barely got enough ranking to be recorded," says Terry. "They gave it a 'five'—the lowest ranking possible to be allowed on one of their recordings—and used it to fill a slot on their CD. One year later, one of their guys wrote to me and said, 'To our amazement, this has become one of our most popular, most requested songs in the past year.'"

From that point on, there was no stopping the song.

"I tell you," says Terry, "God took it from there and began to promote that thing. To this day, we can't believe the testimonies that we get from nations we've never even heard of, from people who've been greatly visited by God's presence as they've sung that song. It's been wonderful to watch the Lord take one of His own songs and use it. It's so simple and so easy to worship with, you don't have to worry about what verse comes next, or a strange key change, or something that maybe only a vocal major could sing. It's just singable. I think that's why people have taken to it like they have."

No matter what the reason, people around the world have, indeed, embraced the song—a blessing made possible by God. He gave to one man the gift of a beautiful little song, and that one man—risking embarrassment and rejection, resisting forces that urged him otherwise—stepped out in obedience to share it.

Story approved by Terry MacAlmon.

15

I Stand in Awe of You

MARK ALTROGGE

"In my fantasies, I was hoping I'd wind up like Keith Green or somebody, doing concerts. . . ."

As a teenage rock 'n roller, Mark Altrogge (pronounced "Al-*troe-ghee*") never anticipated that one day his standard for a song would be its theological soundness.

As a senior pastor and long-time worship leader in the university town of Indiana, Pennsylvania, Mark now values nothing more.

"The ideal song for me to write," he claims, "would be doctrinally rich, yet full of passion and affection for God."

Indeed, it's possible to compose such songs, as Mark demonstrated in such stand-out worship tunes as 1985's "I'm Forever Grateful" and the perennial worship favorite "I Stand in Awe of You," penned in 1986.

"Most of my songs don't have a very impressive story of how I received the inspiration," Mark admits. "It's usually a lot of hard work, hit and miss, playing things over and over, hoping to recognize when something sounds good."

Reflecting on "I Stand in Awe of You," the songwriter says, "I worked on it for quite a while before it clicked." It was the mid-1980s, and Mark, already a husband and father of two (two more children would follow), had become a pastor in Lord of Life Church, affiliated with PDI (*P*roclaiming God's Grace; *D*eveloping Local Churches; *I*nfluencing Our World with the Gospel).

"With most of my songwriting, I'm usually meditating on something by which I'm being affected, either a teaching I've heard or a book I've read. Then I'll try to capture the theme of that meditation in song.

"I'd read the book *The Holiness of God* by R. C. Sproul," he says, "and had been reading books like *The Knowledge of the Holy* by A. W. Tozer. I was affected by God's being infinite and unfathomable in all of His attributes. 'I Stand in Awe of You' was born out of the emotional impact that the doctrine of God's holiness had on me."

The song quickly became a favorite in the circle of PDI churches with which Mark was associated, though it took a bit longer for it to be published. "I had gotten discouraged in the early eighties, sending songs around to publishers," says Mark, "so I began sending three or four songs at a time to some of our churches. I'd say, 'If you can use 'em, go ahead. It's free. I don't want anything for them. I would be honored if any of them just served the church.'"

"I Stand in Awe of You" did, in fact, begin to serve countless believers in worship. Eventually, PDI made the decision to start publishing music, and in 1989 Integrity Music picked up the song for Bob Fitts's *The Lord Reigns*.

Mark recommends this approach to fledgling songwriters. "First of all, see if the song is effective in your own local church," he suggests. "If the song works, then send it out to the family of churches of which you are a part and see if it takes off there. God will get out those songs which He really desires to. It's so important to trust in the Lord's sovereign choice of how He will use us."

In the early 1970s, such talk about God moving would have been foreign to Mark. At that time, his primary focus was on studying art, which he would later teach before becoming a pastor, and playing rock 'n roll, not on doing God's will. When Mark became a Christian in 1974, following graduation, that focus quickly shifted.

"I quit the rock band and wasn't sure what God would have me do with my music. I attempted to write more performance-type songs. In my fantasies, I was hoping I'd wind up like Keith Green or somebody, doing concerts. I know I'm not good enough to do that, but—" He stops, clears his throat, and murmurs dryly: "I was *deceived* into thinking I could at the time."

One distinct spiritual experience during this phase of his life, however, would dramatically alter Mark's plans for the future. "One day, when working on a song, I felt like God said to me, 'Mark, do you want to be a servant with your music?' And I said, basically, 'Yeah, of course.' I then sensed the Lord say to me, 'Write worship songs to serve my people.' That's not to say that other kinds of songs are any less valuable; I just felt like somehow God spoke that to me. Although God may be glorified through many forms of music, He called me in the area of worship.

"At the time I wasn't real excited about worship music. I was used to seeing bands like Yes and Genesis, and their music was really complex. In my arrogance, worship music seemed very elementary. I can remember thinking it would be easy to write a worship song. I found out later it wasn't so easy! My first worship songs were kind of cornball. I wince when I hear them today."

Around this time, Mark began to be discipled by Brent Detwiler, a leader in the PDI church who, in their time together, emphasized doctrine, theology, and character. "I began to have a passion to write songs that had some lyrical depth, some doctrinal depth, and some musical depth that went beyond what I was seeing at the time." Mark was helped and influenced by other PDI leaders as well. The result, he says, was "a desire to write songs that would be strong doctrinally, because I saw that doctrine created affection for God."

Mark himself is a living example of this doctrine-driven affection. Of his goals for the future, he says quietly, "I just want to follow hard after Him and never bring shame to His name." Far from bringing shame to the Lord, Mark's songs are helping to bring God glory as far away as Japan and Malaysia, France and Albania.

"It blows my mind," Mark laughs. "I *never* would have imagined this kind of stuff. To write a song that helps people enter into worship, or to gain deeper understanding, experience, or joy in God's awesomeness, in His beauty and glory—that would be the most satisfying thing I could think of."

He adds thoughtfully, "I couldn't ask for anything more."

16

I Will Call
upon the Lord

MICHAEL O'SHIELDS

"I have only two problems, musically: I can't sing on key and I can't keep time. Otherwise, I do okay."

Michael O'Shields learned the many aspects of ministry the hard way, and perhaps the best way. As a young, itinerant preacher serving a broad stretch of land in west Texas and Oklahoma in the mid-1970s, he got down in the trenches and performed every conceivable type of pastoral task.

Michael had been a Christian for approximately nine years, a pastor for about three, and a husband for just one. Part of a team of eight to nine men, he traveled throughout the region, conducting meetings dedicated to pure Bible teaching.

"In those days, there were no nondenominational churches, really," he says. "People were just hungry for the Word. They would come to these home meetings and we would teach. Then they'd go back to their regular church meetings. There was a real hunger that wasn't being met in the traditional settings."

As a junior member of the ministry team, Michael alternated between leading worship, delivering messages, "passing the hat," and performing any other duty that was required. During this pivotal time in his life, he drew upon an old skill: songwriting.

"I'd written poetry in high school," says Michael. "When I was a junior, we studied English literature and one of the assignments was that everybody had to write a sonnet. Another guy and I had a pretty good trade in sonnets for a while because we could just crank them out. A lot of guys didn't know what to do; they barely understood the concept of iambic pentameter."

It was not Michael's first experience with writing. In fact, the year before, in 1964, a friend had introduced him to Bob Dylan's part-electric, part-acoustic *Bringing It All Back Home* album. "We listened to that and I thought, *You know, I could do this.* That's when I started writing songs. Then when I came to know the Lord, I wrote worship songs."

Michael was still writing worship songs during his term as itinerant pastor.

"I wrote 'I Will Call upon the Lord' because I was driving all over west Texas and Oklahoma. I hadn't been married that long, and finances were tough. Preaching just wasn't paying the way, so we were always praying about the finances. I drove from my home in Oklahoma down to Abilene, Texas—which was two hundred miles—on a Saturday. We had a really good meeting that Saturday night, and I turned around and drove home after the meeting, and the offering was twelve dollars. So I was calling on the Lord!"

The song developed into a type of leader-and-follower format, with the women echoing the men. Although the structure is now commonly used in praise and worship music, in 1975 it was a whole new way of worshiping.

"As far as I know, that was the very first song that was arranged that way," says Michael.

The structure was perfectly designed to meet the needs of the culture to which they were ministering.

"A lot of these meetings were in farming communities," says Michael, "and the men were out in the field all day. They didn't say anything out there and they sure weren't going to say anything when they came in! There was a real revival going on at that time. Usually how it happened was this: The wife got turned on to the Lord and eventually her husband would come on board. We started singing that song so that the men would have to sing first; it required them to take some leadership in worship."

Although Michael had written "I Will Call upon the Lord" and often helped to lead worship, other leaders in his ministry group played a part in making the song a favorite.

"A couple of guys who were musically inclined helped spread

that song. You see, I don't play an instrument and I have only two problems, musically: I can't sing on key and I can't keep time. Otherwise, I do okay."

As Michael's team used "I Will Call upon the Lord" in ministry, and as worshipers took it back to their local churches, the song spread by word of mouth.

Nearly a decade later, Michael was surprised to learn just how far it had traveled.

"In 1983, I was living in a little town called Graham, Texas. We were about one hundred miles from the Dallas-Fort Worth area. One Saturday, I was watching a movie and I went to sleep on the couch. When I woke up, it was about seven o'clock in the morning, and there was the First Baptist Church of Fort Worth singing 'I Will Call upon the Lord' on television as part of their service."

At this point, no one yet knew who had written the song. For a time, this became a stumbling block for Michael.

That same year, he traveled to Dallas for a meeting held by *New Wine* magazine. There were at least three thousand people in attendance. To Michael's surprise, the worship leader led out with "I Will Call upon the Lord."

"They sang it for a half an hour. It was every arrangement that I'd ever heard and some that I hadn't. And everybody there but me was having a great time because, you know, I've got this need for recognition. I wanted to stand up and say, 'Hey! I wrote that song.'"

After the meeting, Michael went back to his hotel. There, a friend who had served as a spiritual mentor to him told him, "Look, you're just going to have to give that to the Lord."

Michael agreed and made a conscious effort to surrender the song back to God.

"I said, 'Look, I don't care if nothing ever happens with this. I just want to be free of it,' and I really got free."

Although the song was written over two decades ago, it continues to be a perennial favorite of worship leaders. In the mid-1980s,

Michael asked a friend who worked at a radio station about the potential life of the song. He was told that a worship album generally has a shelf life of approximately ten years.

"I wrote the song in 1975 and I figured that by 1985, it was about done. But I felt the Lord speak to me, saying, 'No. There's a lot of life left in that song.'"

Indeed, the song continues to be sung in every corner of the world, from the United States to New Zealand to South America, and its popularity shows no sign of waning.

For his part, Michael says he is worried about just one thing.

"Of course, 'I Will Call upon the Lord' is right out of Psalm 18, verses 3 and 46. My biggest concern is that when we all get to heaven, I'm going to meet David and he's going to ask me for half the royalties!"

Whether he's joking or speaking from the heart, Michael acknowledges that his own talent is not what has propelled the song into the hearts of worshipers.

"Even though I wrote the song, I knew it had a life of its own. It's made its own way out into the world. And God just used it. For me, the most satisfying thing is that people all over the world can sing it.

"This is my definition of a good song: one that anyone can sing as if they wrote it themselves. They can make it their own heart cry. Just like the Bible, you can read a Scripture and say, 'Even though David penned *I will call upon the Lord who is worthy to be praised*, I can say that Scripture like I wrote it.'

"And when they sing, they can say, 'That comes right out of my mouth, right out of my heart.'"

Story approved by Michael O'Shields.

17

My Redeemer Lives

EUGENE GRECO

"I saw this commotion over by the pool. I ran over and [my wife] Joy was lying there, kind of shaking."

There are some situations that seem impossible to redeem, such as the painful, life-threatening illness, disrupted ministry opportunity, and ruined family vacation experienced by Eugene Greco's family in 1995. But, as their family of four discovered the hard way, *anything* is possible for our Redeemer.

Both seasoned ordained ministers and trained musicians, Eugene Greco and his wife, Joy, were among a core group of leaders involved with Integrity Music's Worship International conferences in the mid-1990s. When plans were made for a conference to be held in the Hawaiian Islands, the couple decided to take their twelve-year-old daughter and eight-year-old son along and make a family vacation of it. Although the Grecos traveled fairly regularly as a result of ministry opportunities, they had never been to Hawaii and were thrilled by the prospect of the trip.

The roster of the worship conference included both the Grecos' ministry team and hundreds of conference attendees who had signed up for the event. The plan? After arriving in Honolulu, everyone would enjoy a couple of days of sun and fun before the conference formally began.

On their first night in Hawaii, the group was invited to an elaborate luau where they were served such mouth-watering delicacies as raw salmon and poi, among other Hawaiian specialties. Eagerly, ministry team members and attendees filled their plates—and their stomachs—enjoying exotic new tastes and familiar favorites until they could not take another bite.

The next morning, it became clear that something was wrong.

Members of the ministry team, who were supposed to set up for the conference, straggled into breakfast at the hotel. An unusual number of them were not feeling well.

"We realized that it had probably been caused by something we ate the night before," says Eugene. "My wife got *quite* sick and was really feeling lousy."

Like most mothers, Joy did not have time to be sick.

"Our kids were all pumped to go and spend time in the beautiful weather at the pool," says Eugene. "So she said, 'I'll go and just lie down on a beach chair while the kids swim.' I had to go and set up for the meeting. I was ready to go out with my keyboard. All of a sudden, I saw this commotion over by the pool. I ran over and Joy was lying there, kind of shaking."

Joy was rushed to the emergency room. She was not the only one of the group to require treatment that day. One by one, members of the ministry team showed up at area hospitals, but Joy was, by far, in the worst condition.

Curiously, none of the conference attendees became ill; only the ministry team was affected, leading Eugene and others to conclude that this was no simple case of food poisoning. It appeared to be a spiritual warfare attack both against their team and against the practice of praise and worship.

"It was a miserable time," Eugene says. "The illness interfered with some of our ministry time and put a damper on our time there with the kids. Then, when we arrived home—picking up my keyboard at the airport, we discovered the case was damaged. It looked like somebody had taken a crowbar and smashed it. It was like we were getting kicked! We weren't expecting that level of spiritual confrontation, thinking 'Hawaii is part of the United States.' But there was something more to it."

Joy stayed at the hospital for one day, resting and receiving fluids intravenously, before returning to the hotel. The Grecos had hoped to enjoy a couple of vacation days before the time of ministry began; instead, Joy spent most of the trip in bed, recuperating.

Although the doctors had done all they could to help her, she longed for medicine of a different kind.

"While she was in bed," Eugene reports, "she said, 'I'm just starving for a word from God. I need to get into the Word.' But she couldn't read. She couldn't even focus. She was too weak and her body was still shaking."

Eventually, a team member loaned Joy a cassette of Scripture verses put to music. As Joy listened, one particular verse jumped out at her—Isaiah 48:17: "This is what the LORD says—your Redeemer, the Holy One of Israel: 'I am the LORD your God, who teaches you what is best for you, who directs you in the way you should go.'"

"It wasn't so much what the verse said," explains Eugene. "It was how the Lord introduced Himself that struck her. God said to her, 'I am your Redeemer and I will redeem your situation.'"

Joy and Eugene clung to this revelation during her illness. "It was so strong in her spirit," he says. "Whatever bad has come from this, God has promised He's going to turn it around. Something good is going to come out of this. We just don't know what."

After they returned to their home in northern New Jersey, they received notification from the Centers for Disease Control in Atlanta that their Hawaiian feast had been infected with *E. coli* bacteria. This is what had caused Joy's dangerous—and potentially deadly—illness.

By God's mercy, Joy and Eugene both recovered fully. Yet after the family left Hawaii, the revelation that had come in the hotel room remained in the forefront of their minds.

"We went home with a word from God," says Eugene. "It was so real, I said, 'God's going to give me a song from this experience. I know He's going to give me a song about this revelation that Joy received about Him being our Redeemer.'"

Back home in West Milford, New Jersey, Eugene looked up Bible verses about God as Redeemer. "There's such creative power in the Word," Eugene says. "I tell anybody, 'You're going through a dry season creatively? You've got to get into the Word!' It just opens things up."

As he was conducting his research, verse twenty-five from the nineteenth chapter of Job came to mind: "I know that my Redeemer lives, and that in the end he will stand upon the earth." After that everything quickly fell into place.

"It didn't take long for that song to come," says Eugene.

At the time, the Grecos' home base of ministry was a local church in New Jersey, and they were engaged in a traveling music ministry around the states and overseas. After Eugene wrote "My Redeemer Lives," he and Joy used it during their worship times. "We actually ministered with it not knowing *what* God was going to turn out for good."

Then, several months after the Hawaii conference, Eugene and Joy received a thick stack of medical reports in the mail. They also received a surprising offer from the company that had insured the food handlers who were responsible for passing on the *E. coli* bacteria to the team.

"We got a call out of the blue. They said, 'We'd like to compensate you for the pain and suffering that you were caused.' It was a pretty large sum of money."

The company didn't ask the Grecos to sign any type of release. The money they offered was a gift—pure and simple.

It could not have come at a better time.

The previous year, Eugene and Joy had been invited to record a live worship album at a church in Jacksonville, Florida, where they had ministered on several occasions. Convinced that the invitation was God opening a door, yet not knowing from where they'd find the necessary funds for the recording, the Grecos had been moving forward in hopes that it would become a reality.

"We were taking steps of faith, but we didn't have the money. Just when we needed it, this check came and actually covered beyond the need."

That recording was the first to include the song "My Redeemer Lives." Later, well-known worship leader Marty Nystrom, who had also been on the music ministry trip to Hawaii, put the song on the Integrity Music recording, *We Draw Near,* which helped take it to the far corners of the globe.

In retrospect, it's clear that God indeed redeemed the Grecos' disastrous trip to the Islands through the birth of a song, through the provision of finances, through the exalting of praise and worship to God, and through new opportunities for Eugene and Joy to minister to others.

And He performed a work in their hearts.

"Good came out of it," says Eugene. "Whenever we sing that song, I really feel the faith connection: Faith comes by hearing the Word of God. Whatever is affecting me, whenever I hear anything about God being a redeemer, I sense a strong understanding of God's nature, His promise.

"No matter what you experience or what you encounter, God's redemptive power can take what the Enemy meant for evil and bring good out of it. That has become a central revelation in our hearts and ministry, causing our faith to rise to a new level."

Ultimately, the greatest lesson to be learned from the Grecos' story may simply be this: No one can ever silence praise to God.

"It was our vision to bring praise and worship to the islands," says Eugene. On the other hand, "The Enemy meant to stop praise and worship."

But God's power was far greater than anything the Enemy could muster.

"You can't stop praise and worship."

Story approved by Eugene Greco.

18

My Tribute (To God Be the Glory)

ANDRAÉ CROUCH

"He said, 'Andy, I just had this dream. If you read John 17 you'll write a song, . . . and it's going to be one of your biggest songs ever!'"

Andraé Crouch simply wanted to usher brothers and sisters into the family of God. But one of those he ushered gave to him a remarkable prophecy.

Today one of the biggest names in gospel music, Andraé has written some of the most enduring songs used and enjoyed by the church. He has received multiple Dove Awards from the Gospel Music Association and has been inducted into the Gospel Music Hall of Fame.

As children, Andraé and his twin sister, Sandra, were raised by loving Christian parents, who put God above the interests of their family-owned dry cleaning businesses. Andraé clearly remembers that his parents at times shut down operations when an event was happening at the church, and they witnessed to people who came into their cleaning businesses.

In time, Andraé shared his parents' commitment to the Lord. "God blessed me, like my parents, to have a passion for Him and the things of the Lord," Andraé says. "I idolized the way they loved God, and I wanted to be like them. The Scriptures say for us to imitate those who love God. Well, it was very easy for us to imitate our parents, because when they prayed they were *serious.*"

After graduating from high school, Andraé became serious about serving God. In the late 1960s he became music director for Teen Challenge, the ministry of David Wilkerson, author of *The Cross and the Switchblade.* Andraé visited one of Teen Challenge's outreach houses and six months later, while still attending L.I.F.E. Bible College, he took up residence at the house.

"When I was invited to visit there, I knew the Lord was drawing me," says Andraé. "That particular house was right in the heart of L.A. It was a huge mansion, and there were drug addicts there like I'd never seen."

Music was a key part of Andraé's ministry at the house. He started a choir called the Teen Challenge Addicts Choir, and he used music in a variety of other ways.

"I'd go out to witness and take a little keyboard with me to skid row. I was in my heyday!" says Andraé. "The gifts of music that God had given to me, I saw at work firsthand, right on the street. I saw people get saved right on the spot. I saw people weeping before the Lord. I'd never experienced such an outpouring of the Holy Spirit in my life: God using me without my being with my parents or people that I knew."

One of the men who came to the Teen Challenge house for treatment was Larry Reed.

"Larry came into the center when I was there," says Andraé. "He was always threatening to quit the house, saying, 'I'm leaving this place. I don't want nothing to do with God.'"

From the start, Andraé befriended Larry. "Whenever he got edgy, like he was going to leave, I'd say, 'Come on, let's go into the chapel. Let me play some songs for you.' I imitated people he liked to hear and sang my own songs to him. I didn't say all the words all the time; I just played chords for him. He'd say, 'Yeah, I like that, I like that.' So then he'd stay there another day. But I knew that I had to stick with him; I knew my music could hold him there."

Andraé witnessed to Larry, but Larry would say, "Man, I'm sorry. The music is great, but I don't believe all that stuff you're talking about." Andraé didn't push, but would just answer, "That's okay."

One day after Larry had been at the house for about three weeks, Andraé started to sing his song, "The Blood."

"I was playing at chapel, and God gave me some great chords. I started singing, 'the blood will never lose its power,' and I looked at Larry."

Up to this point Larry had not responded to anyone, nor had he responded to any message. "He acted like he wasn't concerned or touched by anything," says Andraé. "But I was singing 'The Blood' from the heart, and the Lord had really anointed me. I happened to look in the audience. Larry was crying, just weeping. I turned my head so he wouldn't see me looking at him, because I knew he'd try to stop. But the Holy Spirit had already touched him."

A couple of days later, Andraé led Larry to the Lord. "He became radical—and *loud!* He was the loudest one in chapel! He'd get up early in the morning and say, *'Glory to God, Hallelujah!'* and wake up everybody. He turned into a guy on fire for God."

After Andraé had been at Teen Challenge for four years, he felt God calling him to move on to other areas of ministry. A couple of months later, Larry, too, left the house after completing his treatment.

Some time later, Andraé heard from his old friend.

"One morning, I got a call from Larry. Larry always called me 'Andy.' He said, 'Andy, I just had this dream. If you read John 17 you'll write a song, and it's going to go all over the world. And it's going to be one of your biggest songs ever!'"

Andraé had his doubts. He wanted to believe what Larry said, but remained skeptical.

"I thought in my spirit, *Okay, Larry, I'll read the Scripture.*" Andraé read from John 17:

When Jesus had finished saying all these things He looked up to Heaven and said, Father the time has come. Glorify your son so he can give glory back to You. . . . I have brought glory to you here on earth by doing everything you told me to do. And now Father, bring me to the glory shared before the world began. . . . My prayer for all of them is that they will be one, just as you and I are one, Father. And just as You are one in me, I am in You. So they will be in us. And the world would believe you sent me. And I have given them the glory you gave me so that they may be as we are. (New Living Translation)

"Larry had told me to read the entire seventeenth chapter of John, so I read it. But I didn't think anything had settled in my spirit. Of course it's a beautiful chapter, but the Holy Spirit was putting something down in me, and I didn't realize it. The next day I wrote 'To God Be the Glory' in about fifteen minutes, not even thinking about what Larry had told me."

Andraé was anxious to share his new song, so he phoned a couple he knew. "I said, 'God just gave me this great song and you guys need to hear it.' They said, 'Come over and sing it for us.' I got there, and after we'd sung the song we started weeping and praising the Lord."

After their time of worship had ended, Andraé told them about hearing from Larry, whom the couple had met while visiting Andraé at the Teen Challenge house.

"I told them, 'Larry told me if I read from Scripture I was going to write a song.'"

Still skeptical, the small group started to laugh off the prophecy, then decided to read the chapter.

Incredulous, they looked at one another.

His friends told him, "*That's* the song, Andraé."

"You're right," he said. "It is."

Just one month later, Andraé was awakened at home at 3:30 A.M. by a phone call from a hospital in southern Oregon. A nurse on the other end of the line told Andraé that one of her patients had asked her to pull out a card from his wallet and call Andraé's number.

Andraé learned that, while driving in his Volkswagen, Larry Reed had been in a head-on collision with a truck. He was not expected to live—was, in fact, on the verge of dying—and he wanted Andraé to know.

Andraé asked to speak to Larry. The nurse wasn't sure if Larry would be able to communicate, but let Andraé try.

"I said, 'Larry. I wrote that song that you told me to.' He said, 'Yeah?' And I said, 'You're gonna be fine. You're gonna be well. Because the Word says "with His blood He has saved me," and He's saved you, and with His power He has raised you. To God be the glory. You're going to be well.'"

> *To God be the glory,*
> *To God be the glory,*
> *To God be the glory,*
> *For the things He has done,*
> *With His blood He has saved me,*
> *With His power He has raised me,*
> *To God be the glory,*
> *For the things he has done.*

Just over a week later, Andraé performed at a scheduled concert at Melodyland Christian Center, near Disneyland. After the performance, he and six friends looked for a particular restaurant. They couldn't find it, however, and wound up by chance at a Denny's restaurant in Anaheim.

"The restaurant was L-shaped, and I was around the corner in the back," says Andraé. "I heard this *'Praise God, Hallelujah!'* I said, 'Boy, that sure sounds like my friend Larry Reed. But that's impossible because he was on the brink of death just about eight to ten days ago.' And do you know what? It was Larry Reed! Larry Reed *well*. God had raised him and he was totally healed."

Still, Andraé remained skeptical about Larry's prophecy regarding the song. Unconvinced, he did not lead with the song when it was recorded for his 1971 *Keep on Singin'* album. The song was recorded instead by his friend Billy Thedford. It's ironic that Andraé did not record the song in his own voice until 1999's *Finally.*

Despite Andraé's early skepticism, "My Tribute" went on to be recorded over five thousand times by various artists. Today it is sung all over the world and is known to many as "The Christian International Anthem."

"I don't feel like I wrote it," says Andraé. "It's not an Andraé Crouch song. I don't even remember *when* I sat down to write it. I just know God funneled it through me. The process of writing it has been banished from my memory because it's His song.

"The song is unique because the inspiration came through another person. It was God [who did it]. He used someone I had invested in, trying to win him to the Lord. [Inspiration came] from the last person I would expect it to come from."

Today, Andraé and his twin sister Sandra—both still single—serve as pastor and assistant pastor of New Christ Memorial Church of God in Christ in San Fernando, California.

"It was God's decision," Andraé says of his move into full-time pastoral ministry. "Like He told Adam and Eve '. . . be fruitful and multiply.' God doesn't subtract, He adds. When I sit down at the piano and turn the tape recorder on, He'll give me something that I can sing to Him. It may be a song that I'll record or I may not record it, but it will be a new song.

"God has been faithful to me to give me music, and now the spoken word as a pastor. My sister is my assistant pastor, and we're having the greatest time of our lives being obedient to God."

As for the future, Andraé says, "We're asking God to keep us close to Him and in the center of His will: obedient to what He chose us to do. I want to be obedient because with obedience is blessing. By blessing I don't mean a pat on the back, I mean I want Him to be pleased with what I do.

"That excites me: to know I'm doing my best to be pleasing to Him."

And when that happens—as at all other times—Andraé gives the glory to God.

19

ONLY BY GRACE

GERRIT GUSTAFSON

"For three years, I heard messages on the grace of God."

As a teenager, Gerrit Gustafson had no idea that he would one day be on fire for God. But since his conversion to Christianity in the late 1960s Gerrit has lived a life with Jesus at the center.

Now a well-known songwriter, worship teacher, and pastor at the beginning of the new millennium, Gerrit still has a heart for music.

A talented saxophone player, in his youth Gerrit largely ignored pop music, favoring instead Dixieland jazz and popular jazz. With the help of his high school band director he put together a group that played local shows and even participated in some USO tours.

"I got addicted to the crowd response," says Gerrit. "I liked what happened when we played for people who appreciated it. So I went to college and majored in music for the first several years."

During his sophomore year at Florida State University, Gerrit providentially met a new roommate. The roommate, in turn, introduced Gerrit to the Lord, and an intensive period of spiritual growth followed. Then Gerrit, who was still majoring in music, came to a crossroads.

"I actually had an issue with the Lord about music. I realized that in my walk with the Lord, music was like an 'Isaac' to me, and He was asking me to let go of it."

In his junior year, Gerrit responded to God's call to change directions and switched his major from music to international affairs. Soon he transitioned into ministry, leading Bible studies and, after graduation, starting a house ministry patterned after the Jesus Movement in southern California.

Gerrit was later ordained by the Baptist church and spent the next two decades involved in pastoral ministry and church planting. Later, he would be at the ground floor of the building of a brand-new music label: Integrity Music. But even in the early days of pastoral ministry, his interest in music remained strong. Ever since becoming a Christian he had been composing songs.

His experience as a pastor, however, completely transformed his approach to writing.

"The music training I'd had was more academic and, for the most part, complicated and not connected to real life, people, emotions, and experiences," he admits. "One of the first places I pastored was in a farming community in Colorado, and a lot of what I knew about music just didn't fly." After that, Gerrit says, "God put me on this track of writing songs that connected to the hearts of ordinary people. Ever since that experience, I've had a real appreciation for the 'ordinary guy.' That's the person I want to serve."

Gerrit's desire to write songs that speak to real life emotions and experiences would lead to the writing of what is today his best-known song. The inspiration came in 1988, during which time Gerrit was traveling and teaching worship conferences as a vocation.

"One of my pastor buddies had served very prominently as a teacher and pastor. Then he developed a problem with alcohol. It was a profound problem, so much so that he left the ministry. He spent several years—probably eight—trying to figure out how to overcome the problem. He went through discouragement after discouragement and almost lost his family. He went to various kinds of Christian ministries to find help, and he never really did.

"Finally he found help in an AA clinic in Minnesota. The man there really challenged him that he was a religious phony. No one had ever gotten to that level with my friend. The man said, 'You're not honest with God.'"

Confronted with the harsh realities of his situation, the friend received a profound revelation of the grace of God—and what it means to have an honest relationship with Him.

Gerrit and another pastor walked this friend through the process of ultimately being restored to ministry. As part of the process, Gerrit committed three years of his life to helping the man launch a new church, where Gerrit served as worship leader.

This redeemed pastor's experience with God's grace powerfully influenced the tone and message of the church.

"For three years," Gerrit says, "I heard messages on the grace of God from this grateful pastor who had been restored."

Gerrit kept this message of unrelenting grace in mind when he sat down to write songs. One night he came home from work and sat down at the piano, where he experimented with one of his favorite chords.

"I love the feel of a major chord with an added second," he says. "I love a melody that uses the fifth and the second. I played the first line of the melody a thousand times before the song began to go anywhere. The melody came first, but I knew it was going to be about God's grace contrasted with human effort. I liked the phrase in Galatians, 'human endeavor.'

"Most of the songs I write have a Scripture reference. There was also the passage about '. . . who would stand if you would mark our transgressions?' in Psalm 130:3. So Galatians and Psalms are the Old Testament/New Testament anchor points of the song."

> *Only by grace can we enter,*
> *Only by grace can we stand.*
> *Not by our human endeavor*
> *But by the blood of the Lamb.*
> *Into Your presence You call us;*
> *You call us to come*
> *Into Your presence; You draw us*
> *And now by Your grace we come.*

Now by Your grace we come.
Lord if You mark our transgressions
Who will stand?
Thanks to Your grace we are cleansed
By the blood of the Lamb.

Gerrit spent about three weeks developing "Only by Grace."

"I remember loving to sing it!" he says. "I often get locked into a song and it will be my song for a period of two or three months."

At that time, he was working with worship leader and songwriter Graham Kendrick on the Hosanna recording *Amazing Love*, and "Only by Grace" quickly landed a spot on the recording. Graham helped to make the song a huge success in England, where for a time it was even more popular than it was in the United States. As satisfying as it was to see the song this well received, however, Gerrit finds far greater satisfaction in the impact it has on believers around the world.

"The greatest honor in my life came through a conversation with a mentor, Jim Reed. He's ministered in China over the years and he was in Taiwan where everything was in Chinese, including the worship songs. One day he was listening to the worship. He didn't know most of the songs, but he heard this song and said, 'I know that song!' Sometimes the melodies of songs get lost in different languages, but it came to him that it was 'Only by Grace' in Chinese. He asked the leaders where they'd learned it, and they said they had learned it from mainland Chinese believers.

"What struck me was the picture of these little underground churches in mainland China singing that song that got plucked out in my living room in 1988. I don't know where they got it; as far as I know it has never been recorded in China. But that song had been used in those little meetings—some of them illegal. I can't think of a greater privilege in life than to have provided those brothers and sisters with something to give expression to their hearts."

Nothing could please Gerrit more, for he has long seen himself not primarily as a songwriter, pastor, and worship leader, but as a servant.

"A long time ago God did something to my heart. He challenged me in this way: Music is not primarily about self-expression; it is about helping people to worship. The idea that came to my mind was, 'Gerrit, I want you to take up the towel and the basin of water and serve the body of Christ.' That means finding those songs that God is truly blessing and giving them place.

"I'm still fascinated by the power of simple, people songs."

Story approved by Gerrit Gustafson. "Only by Grace" by Gerrit Gustafson, © 1990 Integrity's Hosanna! Music/ASCAP, c/o Integrity Media, Inc., 1000 Cody Road, Mobile, AL 36695.

20

Open the Eyes of My Heart

PAUL BALOCHE

"Following Christ . . . is much more than music; . . . music is the by-product of living for Christ."

ccording to acclaimed songwriter Paul Baloche, the best songs are not those crafted purposefully through human skill; they're the ones birthed out of a heart naturally overflowing with praise.

And he should know. One of the most respected music producers, prolific songwriters, and well-known and well-loved worship leaders in the church today, Paul has recorded and produced an impressive number of praise and worship projects and has worked with a wide range of artists, from easy listening's John Tesh and Michael W. Smith to Christian rock's Sonicflood. A producer for Integrity Music, Paul has also produced four albums for Maranatha! Music's Praise Band and is a successful recording artist in his own right.

In fact, since the 1970s, Paul has lived a life that is filled with music.

For a time, growing up in New Jersey and Pennsylvania, Paul thought that he might be called to the priesthood. Instead, as a young adult he found himself making a living as a rock musician, playing late into the night at East Coast hot spots.

Although Paul made a name for himself on the club scene, his success left him dissatisfied and unfulfilled. Eager to experience something more, Paul set out to fill the emptiness in his soul, and in December of 1980, he had a born-again experience that would change his life forever.

Soon Paul, still a single young man, moved to the West Coast to attend music school. There, he met two songwriters who would prove to be influential in both his musical and spiritual life.

"I went to California and that's where I met Kelly Willard. I didn't really even know who she was," he says of the woman who wrote such worship favorites as "Cares Chorus" and "Make Me a Servant."

Paul was attracted in a big way to Christian music. "I thought, *Man, that's cool: to be able to do pop music that's about God.* I'd never heard such a thing growing up in Philadelphia."

Paul spent a great deal of time with Kelly, her husband Dan, and their children. "I'd go to their house on weekends and hang out and play with their kids and mow the lawn. It was fun to hang around with a family and just be around them. I'd go with Kelly to some of the concerts and sell records."

Kelly and Dan were influential in the early Maranatha! Music period. But they influenced Paul, too. "I learned a lot from them about humility and transparency and being authentic. I saw that really following Christ in your life and in your family is much more than music; that music is the by-product of living for Christ; that songs become an overflow of your life."

A second mentor who took Paul under his wing during this time was Lenny LeBlanc, author of such tunes as "There Is None Like You" and co-writer with Paul of the song "Above All." After Paul met and married his wife, Rita, his own songwriting also took off.

"Rita had had a born again experience similar to mine. She was writing new songs, and I had never written much. I'd just been a guitar player. I'd send Kelly our songs and she'd say, 'Oh, that's really great.'"

As Paul's songwriting developed, so did his career in the music ministry. In 1990 he began leading worship at Community Christian Fellowship. He also became involved in the ministry of Youth with a Mission, working with Jimmy and Carol Owens, and leading overseas worship schools in such places as Singapore and South Africa. He recorded his first live worship project, *He Is Faithful,* with Integrity Music in 1992.

In 1997 came the most pivotal songwriting experience of Paul's life. The writing followed the pattern common to the creation of many of his songs.

"For me, a lot of songs come out of worship times when I'm praying with a guitar in my hand," he says. "At our church, it's not uncommon for me to play one or two chords as people are getting prayed for. I just begin to sing out some prayers."

Throughout the mid-1990s, Community Christian Fellowship operated under a climate of revival. Together, the congregation and its leaders were praying for renewal at numerous worship nights and prayer meetings. As the worship leader, Paul sometimes led worship for almost two hours at a time, throughout periods of intercessory prayer.

One morning, while standing at the front of the church, leading worship, the phrase "Open the eyes of my heart" suddenly sprang to mind.

"I'd heard a pastor pray that a couple of years before, and I had written it in my journal. I liked the way it sounded. He said something like, 'Lord, we ask you to open the eyes of our hearts, to help us to see into your Word tonight.' He kind of blew by it, but it really struck me. Later I looked into Ephesians 1:18 and spent some time there, praying that."

On the morning that "Open the Eyes of My Heart" was written, Paul was—as usual—singing out prayers as men and women were being ministered to at the end of the church service.

"Oh, Lord, we ask you to come right now and touch our hearts, Jesus," he prayed out loud, strumming his guitar. At that moment, he says, "That phrase popped into my mind: 'Open the eyes of our hearts, Lord.' Open our eyes, Lord. We want to see You."

> *Open the eyes of our hearts, Lord;*
> *Open the eyes of our hearts.*
> *We want to see You.*
> *We want to see You.*

"You know when you think, 'Yeah, that feels right'? At the time, I didn't think, 'Boy, that sounds like a good song!' I just thought, 'Yeah, yeah, Lord, that's our prayer right now.' It felt like the sincere prayer of our hearts at that moment.

"I sang that through a few times and people started singing along with me. I don't know how the other part came about. I think I was thinking about when Isaiah saw the Lord: 'Lord, to see You high and lifted up. It's just shining. It's shining so bright, Lord. Shining in the light of Your glory.' I was saying these phrases and my sound man always keeps the 'record' button on because you never know. . . .

"Those are moments I try to capture because it rings true," he says, proving how completely the lessons from Kelly Willard have hit home. "I'd much rather stumble upon a song idea in the midst of worship or prayer than when sitting in a room trying to come up with clever hooks. It's more honest because it springs from the act of worship, instead of saying, 'Okay, I've got to write some cool Christian worship chords.' You end up with a Christian jingle. I've written those and I'm not proud of those. I'd rather be in a place of worship and let songs come as a by-product."

Later that week, Paul listened to the tape of the spontaneous version of "Open the Eyes of My Heart." There in his office, he says, "I took that idea, which was mostly written as a prayer, and sanded the edges so that it could be a simple little prayer song."

In the following weeks, Paul taught the finished song to the church, as he has done with so many of his and Rita's songs, many of which have ultimately landed on Integrity Music recordings.

"Rita and I feel like that's our role," he says. "We try to write songs for our church. I'm always thinking about, 'What do we as a church need to say to God?' I'm aware that we have the privilege and the awesome task of putting into the mouth of God's children the words that they can sing to Him. It's much like a greeting card: I'm not sure how to say that I love my wife again on Valentine's Day. I go to the card store and I look through several until I find a card that makes me say, 'Wow, that's neat! I never thought of saying it that way.'

"As we sing to God, it changes our lives and has the potential to change our hearts, our marriages, our families, our communities. The ripple effect of a song amazes me. Somebody once said, 'We'll remember maybe ten sermons in our lives but we'll remember hundreds of songs.'

"People ask me, 'Did you know "Open the Eyes of My Heart" would become a big song?' Definitely not. They all feel good when they first come out, sounding honest and natural."

As Paul continued to sing "Open the Eyes of My Heart," people immediately grabbed onto it. "It really meant something to them," says Paul. "Maybe it's our desire: We've been Christians a long time, and we're frustrated with ourselves for lack of growth, and we say, 'I want to be changed, God.'

"When people have an encounter with the Lord, they see Him. It seems like the prayer of our hearts is, 'I don't want to just learn about You, talk about You; I want to *see* You. I want to become more aware of You actually working in my life, in my family, in the world.'

"You don't have to be a 'songwriter' to write songs to the Lord. Just sing your prayers.

"That's where the best songs come from."

Story approved by Paul Baloche. "Open the Eyes of My Hear" by Paul Baloche, © 1997 Integrity's Hosanna! Music/ASCAP, c/o Integrity Media, Inc., 1000 Cody Road, Mobile, AL 36695.

21

Pass It On

KURT KAISER

"The thought occurred to me,
Isn't it amazing what can happen
if you take your hands off the
ability God has given you and
watch what happens?"

It only takes a spark to get a fire going. . . ."

During the Jesus Movement of the early 1970s, Kurt Kaiser's simple, sweet youth song, "Pass It On," hit the bull's eye for evangelicals. The words captured perfectly the passion of a newly redeemed generation, and it was an ideal fit for the musical parlance of its time. The song became foundational to the praise and worship music we enjoy today.

Like the flames of the campfires around which it was sung, and like the flames of renewal itself, "Pass It On" spread like wildfire. In 1970, such excellent and effective songs were rare, and people were eager to enjoy the piece and . . . well, "pass it on."

Years later, worshipers still get a lump in their throats when they sing it.

> . . . That's how it is with God's love,
> once you've experienced it—
> you spread His love to everyone,
> you want to pass it on.

"If you write just a couple of things that people will remember or sing through the years," Kurt Kaiser muses today, "maybe that's all that's required of a person."

Kurt, however, has written more than just "a couple" of songs that will long be remembered. He has, in fact, copyrighted more than two hundred songs, including "Pass It On" and the popular "Oh, How He Loves You and Me," and has written many more.

With characteristic humility, he admits, "I'd give a lot to write another 'Oh, How He Loves You and Me,' or another 'Pass it On,' but I'm sixty-six years old, and I don't think it's going to happen. But I keep writing."

Kurt's love of Christian music began at a young age. It's appropriate, since "Pass It On" is so often sung *a cappella*, that he was first introduced to musical praise and worship through the unaccompanied singing at the Plymouth Brethren church in which he was raised. Yet not long after his high school graduation, the musically talented young man soon was traveling across the country as an accompanist.

"Those were great times for me," he remembers. "But then somebody said, 'Kurt, you need to go to college.' The man was a trumpet player and a missionary, and he said, 'When my lip goes . . . I'm finished. There's nothing else I am equipped to do.' That was the best advice I ever got."

Kurt followed the advice and enrolled at the American Conservatory in Chicago and at Northwestern University, from which he earned undergraduate and graduate degrees. During these years, he studied piano and received extensive training in both classical tradition and hymnody.

In 1959, Kaiser brought these skills to Word Music in Waco, Texas, where he served first as Director of Artists and Repertoire, then as Vice President and Director of Music. Throughout the 1960s, he was in great demand, writing orchestrations for artists like Jerome Hines, Anita Bryant, Burl Ives, Tennessee Ernie Ford, and many others. While he enjoyed this work, he felt a burden to use music somehow to touch young people with the good news of the gospel.

He talked to his friend, arranger/composer Ralph Carmichael, in 1969 about collaborating on a project aimed at youth.

Kurt said, "Ralph, let's do something that really makes it for kids." Ralph liked the idea, and suggested the two brainstorm separately and combine their ideas later.

"I asked him about continuity and he said that we shouldn't worry about continuity, and it wasn't important anyway. It was very good advice."

This collaboration soon led to the creation of the musical "Tell It Like It Is."

"We were almost finished with the project, and I met with Ralph in Tulsa. We assigned each other final responsibilities. My job was to write a 'Just As I Am' for young people. The tune came the following Sunday night after church; I was sitting in my den at home and a little fire burned in the fireplace. It was in the wintertime. I looked into the fire and the thought came to me, '. . . it only takes a spark to get a fire going—and soon all those around. . . .'

"Once the second line had been written—'That's how it is with God's love'—it helps set the pace for the entire poem. At that point my wife Pat said, 'Sweetheart, why don't you say something about shouting it from mountains?' That's where the line came from, 'I'll shout it from the mountaintop, I want my world to know; the Lord of love has come to me, I want to pass it on.'"

After completing the song, Kurt stepped outside into the cold and rain. "Pat and I walked down to the end of our street and back, and I felt good about the tune. The next day I called Ralph. He said, 'Oh yeah, Kurt! That'll sing!'" Kurt laughs. "And it really has. It's amazing how it's worked."

Amazing indeed. Kurt once watched on TV as "a hundred-thousand people at the Cotton Bowl were singing my song. They were lighting candles off of one another. The camera would first pick up maybe five thousand people and then pull back and pick up fifteen thousand. The whole place was filled with people singing,

'. . . it only takes a spark to get a fire going. . . .' The thought occurred to me, *Isn't it amazing what can happen if you take your hands off the ability God has given you and watch what happens?*"

Over the years, the song has been sung in submarines, at the Sea of Galilee, and at countless camps. "A man who was killed in a gas station holdup had been part of a group who sang 'Tell It Like It Is.' The kids in the group, who meant everything to this person, sang 'Pass It On' at his funeral." From waiters to fellow travelers on planes, Kurt constantly meets those who have felt the impact of the song. He says, "People sometimes admit to having heard the song too often."

"One time Bev [George Beverly] Shea and his wife, Karlene, were here in Waco having lunch with Pat and me, and the waiter was a rather young guy. He said, 'I'm trying to earn some money so that my fiancée and I can get married.' So Bev Shea says, 'Have you chosen the music for your wedding? Do you know the song 'Pass It On?' The waiter said, "I'm sick and tired of 'Pass It On'! Then Bev Shea pointed to me and said, 'He wrote that song!' The guy never cracked a smile. He said, 'Every camp I've been to, it's always . . . 'Pass it On!'

"We had a lot of laughs about that one!" Kurt remembers with a grin.

Yet despite its extensive use—perhaps even because of it—the impact remains. And Kurt himself continues to influence the praise and worship movement. He has worked with artists like Christopher Parkening and Kathleen Battle, and songwriting is an important part of his life; his songs range from contemporary collaborations, written with artists like Billy Crockett, to setting music to selections from the Book of Common Prayer. Yet despite his involvement in a new generation of praise and worship music, Kurt's love for the classics remains. He reminds worship leaders not to lose sight of their musical and spiritual heritage.

He witnessed the effect of an old hymn at an outdoor worship event several years ago. "They were playing Isaac Watts's hymn, 'At the Cross,' and sitting in front of me was Barry McGuire," Kurt says. "When it was finished, Barry turned around to me, and he was absolutely sobbing.

"He said, 'Who wrote that tune, man?' I told him that hymn has been around for a couple hundred years. 'No way!' he said. It was so moving for him, and I'll always remember that."

In recent years, Kurt was given an opportunity to teach a course on hymn writing at a creativity conference.

At the conference, Kurt says, "I asked one lady to recite the text from the praise chorus, 'Alleluia.' So she said, 'Alleluia, alleluia, alleluia, alleluia,' and then she quit. I said, 'No, that's only half of it. Now do the second half.'

"She said, 'Alleluia, alleluia, alleluia, alleluia.'

"'Now,' I said to a friend of mine who teaches voice, 'would you please recite the text to the hymn, 'When I was sinking down, sinking down beneath . . .' ("What Wondrous Love Is This," lyrics attributed to Alexander Means).

"Even though some of the praise choruses are very, very pretty, I don't want leaders who are between the ages of twenty-five and fifty to give up the old hymns that have something to say and replace them with choruses that are oftentimes just repetitive. That really troubles me: to abandon the hymnal for the sake of expediency.

"Do not abandon the hymns," Kurt urges. "There's so much marvelous theology in hymnody, and it's lost to at least one generation, and maybe more now."

22

THE RIVER IS HERE

ANDY PARK

"I called my wife, Linda, and told her that it was a fun song, it had energy. Yet even I was wondering, Will this song work?"

A picture is worth a thousand words. A picture is also worth a thousand hearts—or perhaps millions—filled with praise. For in the early 1990s, God used a simple pictorial image to inspire the writing of what has become one of the church's most popular worship songs.

At the time, great spiritual renewal was sweeping through churches in the United States, England, and many other parts of the world.

In the midst of this tremendous growth, Andy Park—then serving as worship pastor at the Anaheim Vineyard Christian Fellowship—saw in his mind's eye a great mountain with a river flowing down its slopes and through its valleys. It was a picture that remained with him for many days.

"I didn't know at that time that God meant for it to be a song," says Andy. He responded to the vision by conducting a simple Bible word study, looking up related Scriptures in Revelation, Ezekiel, and the Psalms, immersing himself in the river-and-mountain analogy.

At around this time, Andy went away on a two-day retreat devoted to prayer and writing. There, in the little retreat center where he had hidden himself away, the song "The River Is Here" sprang to life.

"It's a style I don't write in a lot," says Andy. "Musically, it goes to my roots, which are folk and country rock, and it was easy to adapt it to the Celtic feeling. But at the time I had no idea how it would be received. I had no idea that it would become a well-known song."

While many contemporary praise and worship songs follow a simple verse, chorus, and bridge format, Andy quickly saw that he had enough material to write three full verses.

"In writing the song, I swapped lines from different verses and experimented with combining different lines in different verses. It seemed like there was enough solid content there to make it work. When you do a little bit of digging in the Scripture and find good solid content, it's worth extending a song to more than two verses. Not to say that every word is straight from the Bible; a lot of it is definitely an adaptation of Scripture."

The song came together quickly, and was finished in about two hours.

"I called my wife, Linda, afterward and told her that it was a fun song, it had energy. Yet even I was wondering, *Will this song work?* I didn't know."

The song did work. Perfectly, in fact. Particularly in light of the renewal Andy's church was experiencing at the time.

"There was a real energy for worship—higher than average anticipation—in that period," he recalls. "When people came to church, they were ready to worship. There was an anticipation that God was moving and He was going to do things. So the theme of the song fit that season of our church's life, because of course it talks about the presence of God—or the River—being here now. It talks about the believer's ability to come to the river, go up to the mountain, and find the Lord. All I have to do is play the intro; people immediately know what's coming, so wherever I go, people start celebrating because they know the River is here."

Down the mountain the river flows
And it brings refreshing wherever it goes.
Through the valleys and over the fields
The river is rushing and the river is here.

The river of God sets our feet a-dancing,
The river of God fills our hearts with cheer;
The river of God fills our mouths with laughter
And we rejoice for the river is here.

A 1995 Vineyard recording of the same name launched "The River Is Here" on its journey to believers around the globe. The song continues to stir hearts from every nation—and even from different faiths.

"I've done some ministry in Madras, India," says Andy, "a large Hindu school there with ten thousand students. They adopted 'The River Is Here' for their theme song for a whole year, even though it was a Hindu school! That was funny, you know, but really wonderful. They sang it in all their school assemblies."

The river of God is teeming with life,
And all who touch it can be revived.
And those who linger on this river's shore
Will come back thirsting for more of the Lord.

At the Anaheim Vineyard, Andy worked directly with senior pastor John Wimber, author of the classic praise song, "Isn't He?" During their time together, John impressed upon his staff the importance of directing hearts not to personal ministries and those who lead them, but to the God those ministries and people are intended to glorify.

"John told the story of a pastor asking him for advice on 'my ministry,' as in, 'How can I make my ministry grow?' And John said to the guy, 'You don't have a ministry. It's *Jesus*' ministry. None of us have our own ministry. We're all just participating in *His* ministry.' John was saying that ministry is not about any one individual's influence. It's about 'How can the kingdom be established and how can God be glorified' regardless of whose name is on the song or on the sign, or whose name is identified with a service or project."

Andy left the Anaheim Vineyard to serve at a Vineyard Fellowship in British Columbia. Now senior pastor of the North Langley Vineyard, Andy continues to be influenced by the teachings of his former pastor and mentor.

"John's biggest contribution in worship and imparting worship had to do with intimacy with God—in knowing God through musical worship as opposed to putting on a program that the church will simply listen to.

"Worship is a means by which God makes Himself known to us, where we become vulnerable to God and He speaks to us, encourages us, and convicts us of sin. We actually see God: not just on a mental level, not just on a cognitive level, but by the revelation of the Spirit. Nothing can take the place of personally encountering God. He pours out His love, and then Christianity becomes not just a doctrine that people hold to, it becomes real. It becomes experiential, like it was for Paul.

"And then anything can happen."

> *Up to the mountain we love to go*
> *To find the presence of the Lord.*
> *Along the banks of the river we run,*
> *We dance with laughter giving praise to the Son.*

23

Sometimes Alleluia

CHUCK GIRARD

"Every time the phone rang, we thought it was God!"

If life was a computer screen, a click on the name "Chuck Girard" would link to lots of treasures. Any discussion of the Jesus Movement, early contemporary Christian music, the band Love Song, Calvary Chapel, Chuck Smith, Maranatha! Music—even surf music and "Little Honda"—will eventually lead to the sandy-haired musical pioneer.

If you wade through all that excitement, though, Chuck Girard emerges best known for a simple and beautiful worship song called "Sometimes Alleluia." The chorus is a quiet, awestruck observation that, although our praises may take different forms, adoration for Christ should make up the central theme of our lives. The less-heard verses are a call to worship Him boldly, that those "outside these walls" might know Him, too.

The birth of "Sometimes Alleluia" is best understood within the context of Chuck's own spiritual journey.

In the late 1960s, Chuck had been trying to fill the void within him, unsatisfied with record contracts, drugs, and in his words, "wine, women, and song."

His search ended at the feet of Jesus, in a "little country church on the edge of town," known as Calvary Chapel in Costa Mesa, California. It was 1970, and the rapidly growing ministry, fueled by fires of revival, was a spiritual greenhouse. Consider the intensity of that greenhouse effect: A few months before, Chuck and his friends, Tommy Coomes and Fred Field, had nearly gone to jail for drug possession; now, with Jay Truax, they stepped onto the Calvary Chapel stage and defined what was soon to be called Jesus Music. The group was named Love Song.

For the next four years, Love Song recorded heartfelt, ground-breaking songs. Uncompromising Christian lyrics saddled up a pleasing blend of folk, pop, rock, and country styles. That music was, and remains, widely embraced. At one point, *CCM Magazine* named Love Song's 1972 debut as the number-7, all-time best contemporary Christian recording. With three hundred thousand copies in print—unprecedented at the time—a media wave thrust the album and young Christians who recorded it into a high pressure, high visibility role.

The band worked hard, maybe too hard. Chuck says, "Every time the phone rang, we thought it was God!" As a result, they played as often as the laws of physics would allow; it wasn't unusual for the band to set up, play, and tear down three times in a single day.

Recognizing an impending burn-out, a friend at Calvary Chapel (Love Song's home base) arranged a private get-away for the group at a cabin at Lake Big Bear, east of Los Angeles. Chuck, his new wife, Karen, Mike Macintosh, and couple of band members went.

"We gathered around the living room and built a fire in the fireplace; we were going to worship," says Chuck. We had guitars up there and just started to sing the Calvary Chapel/Maranatha!-type songs." Chuck says he didn't know very much about spontaneous singing at the time, but as he puts it, "somehow, this chorus was birthed."

"All we had was the chorus," Chuck explains. "We sang it and used it as a vehicle for our worship that night, and then I forgot about it." He figuratively put the song on the shelf "and went about my life."

In late 1973, it was obvious that Love Song would soon be disbanding. Many internal reasons led to the dissolution of the group, but Chuck summarizes that "the pressure and responsibility of the visibility we had in those days took a toll on us."

He began to assemble material for a solo album, which eventually became his self-titled recording. He wanted to close the project with a worship song, and Karen remembered the simple song written at Big Bear. In those days his understanding of praise and worship was nominal, and he considered the song too simplistic. Chuck said, "'Naw, . . . I need a real song.' It was just three chords. It was something we used just up there. I dismissed it as second-string because I didn't realize, as I do now, that a worship song is birthed in a time of actually worshiping God. Such songs come from the heart and they come out of a worship experience." Karen, however, recognized what was happening and encouraged Chuck to go to the Lord and finish the song.

"I'm one of those husbands who listens to his wife's instincts," explains Chuck. "I sat down at the piano, and wrote all the verses in about fifteen minutes. The words just poured out."

The Second Chapter of Acts provided backup vocals in the beautiful finished recording. Christian Music Executive Billy Ray Hearn, just starting Sparrow Records at the time, was in the studio and commented that the song would probably become a standard.

"After it was released, Jimmy Swaggart picked it up and it was the theme song for his TV show for all the years he was on," Chuck says. "It's my most well-known song and it's been recorded the most."

Chuck adds an interesting footnote to the story: "Years later, I was introduced to the writings of Charles Spurgeon, and was reading his sermons for the first time. I read the line 'Oh let our joy be unconfined, let us sing with freedom unrestrained.' This was a verbatim line from 'Sometimes Alleluia'! It was staggering to me, and I thought, 'Well *that's* the Holy Spirit!'"

24

THE SWEETEST NAME OF ALL

TOMMY COOMES

"The goal was to find some fumbling way to tell God how great He is."

Today, the name of Tommy Coomes can't be separated from the praise and worship movement, which hit its stride in the early 1970s. But back then, Tommy was not yet a spiritual or musical leader. He was simply trying to find his way.

Having just finished a tour of duty in the army, Tommy came home and was reconnecting with some musician friends he once had played with in local bars and clubs. In March of that year, he met the Lord at Calvary Chapel of Costa Mesa. At the time it was a small church community of approximately two hundred people, but it had an outreach as big as its members' hearts.

Like many other young men and women living in southern California at the time, the former college music major became a product of the Jesus Movement. "All these young kids were getting saved left and right," Tommy says. "The enthusiasm was for—number one—finding out that God's love was real, then for reading the Bible. It was great! The Word of God was the central focus, and we all read it and went to church every night. The church was open seven nights a week."

Around this time, Tommy hooked up with three friends—Chuck Girard, Jay Truax, and Fred Field—to form the group Love Song. (Drummer John Mehler joined later.) The band was soon playing regularly at local coffee houses, clubs, churches, and youth gatherings. Made up of four guys who had come out of the bars and clubs of the drug culture, Love Song was soon adopted by a couple of retired schoolteachers who took their story to heart. "Their kids had been saved from drugs and were off in the ministry somewhere, and the parents invited us to live in their house with them."

The band accepted the couple's offer, and a profound songwriting experience soon followed in that home.

"It was late at night," Tommy says, "and I was lying on a little bunk bed, reading Revelation for the very first time. I got to the Scripture where the angels are casting down their crowns before the glassy sea and singing 'Holy, Holy, Holy' and 'Lord God Almighty' and 'Who Was and Who Is and Who Is to Come.' I got so excited about this scene!

"God might as well have just turned on a tape recorder, because I heard it as clear as a bell! I didn't have a tape recorder to record the idea, so I jumped out of bed and grabbed the guitar, figured out the basic melody, and wrote down the lyrics as fast as I could.

"I got up the next morning, took it to church, and asked our pastor if I could sing the song. As I sang, he bowed his head and appeared to be overwhelmed. Little did I know that he had been praying for some kind of new music in the church. It was a sign to him—and to me, too—that 'God is at work here.' God hears our prayers and wants to do something new and fresh."

That song, "Holy, Holy, Holy" landed a spot as the only worship song on the very first album produced by Maranatha! Music. Maranatha! had been conceived of and launched at Calvary Chapel by pastor Chuck Smith, who wanted to help the young artists in his congregation earn "gas money" that would allow them to continue their music ministry. The album *Maranatha I*—was then officially titled *The Everlastin' Living Jesus Music Concert*.

"Is that the worst title you've ever heard?" Tommy laughs.

The song enjoyed tremendous success throughout the 1970s. Love Song drew bigger and bigger crowds, and numerous songwriting credits quickly followed. At the same time, Tommy started producing praise albums for Maranatha!—work he would continue throughout the 1980s and 1990s. But he is perhaps best known for the songs "As We Gather," which he co-wrote with Mike Faye, and "The Sweetest Name of All," arguably the most popular of Tommy's tunes.

"The Sweetest Name of All" was written a decade after Tommy penned his first praise song, and it made its debut on *Praise IV*, along with such praise and worship classics as "In His Time" and "I Love You, Lord." "The Sweetest Name of All" became an indisputable hit, but at the time he wrote it, Tommy was feeling anything but successful.

"My life was at a low. I focused on all the ways I had failed God, and I was overwhelmed with how gracious and patient He is and had been with me. I looked at all the goals I'd had for my life, and I felt like a failure. I produced a lot of albums in those days, stayed up late at night, drank a lot of coffee, and didn't sleep much. So I was probably exhausted."

Tommy was haunted by what he calls the "shoulda-oughta-gotta list," torturing himself by thinking about all the things he felt he should be doing for Jesus. "I focused on a few things that I'd done really well on. But I felt like other parts of my life were not so good. I think a lot of people that are very successful feel this. One day I sat down at the piano, and I felt overwhelmed by how great and patient God is and how small and insignificant I am. The song was my spontaneous prayer of praise at that moment: 'Jesus, you're the sweetest name of all.'

"It wasn't meant to be a song at all; it was a moment of frustration. I began to weep, and I thought, *Oh my, this is a really pretty melody. This is a really nice song.* And I had to get out paper, in the middle of my worship and sobbing and devotions, to write it down, because I knew something good was happening. But the goal was to find some fumbling way to tell God how great He is.

"I couldn't write fast enough, it flowed so well. But then I had to deal with rhymes and arrangements at the same time. The whole thing happened in about an hour. It was very quick—a lot of songs have taken me five years to write."

The song quickly landed on Maranatha's *Praise IV* album. Following the quieter success of the *Praise I, II,* and *III* albums, *Praise IV* broke through to the wider church in denominations all across America. Tommy says, "It's probably the highest selling *Praise* album we've ever produced."

Years later, Tommy still marvels at the message of "The Sweetest Name of All."

"What an incredible God," says Tommy. "He accepts us right where we are, even if we're ten years into our Christian walk and feel like a failure. It realigns our hearts to realize how great and how patient He is. One of my favorite verses, Romans 2:4, says something like, 'Don't you know? It's the goodness of God that leads us to repentance.'

"A lot of times in the Christian faith, we act like we're not human. We act as though we don't have needs. Francis Schaeffer said that the main difference between a Christian and a non-Christian is that the Christian has chosen to cast himself upon God's solution for his problem.

"I think that's one of the reasons why the song grabs people: because it's talking about human need and how God is so faithful to meet us in our time of need."

Story approved by Tommy Coomes.

25

TAKE MY LIFE

SCOTT UNDERWOOD

"It was originally called the 'Fisherman's Song.'"

God can use even camping songs to carry choice bits of truth to His people.

Scott Underwood's "Take My Life" is such a song, written—using just three guitar chords—to the splashing of a northern California lake. It has since found its way from the tackle box into hearts everywhere. Whether played by a single guitarist at a campfire or a full band in the sanctuary, "Take My Life" always seems to work. The lyrics are a prayer of yielding to the Lord's will, layered with a catchy melody over a simple rhythm.

Scott, author of dozens of fine praise songs, laughs when he tells the story of how he wrote it.

"It was originally called the 'Fisherman's Song,'" he chuckles. "We were at a men's retreat in the early 90s. I was fishing with a good friend of mine named John Woodhouse. John loves fishing. After the Lord and John's wife, I think fishing may come third in his list of loves—maybe a close third."

Besides the bait, John had brought along a guitar.

Scott says he doesn't usually strum around campfires and at picnics, but this day he made an exception.

"Nothing was biting," he says. "I resisted for a while, but pretty soon I picked up the guitar and started playing."

Almost immediately, he was singing.

> *Take my heart and form it;*
> *take my mind, transform it;*
> *take my will, conform it to Yours. . . .*

"It was just that fast," he remembers. "And I thought, 'Lord, surely somebody has taken those thoughts and put them together in a rhymed way before.' But I couldn't recall having heard it."

Within minutes, he'd added the verse, "Holiness, holiness, is what I long for. . . ."

Scott played the fledgling song for John and asked his opinion.

"John is a big burly guy, just a wonderful man, and he said, 'I think you've got something there.' Then he started to cry! He's a tenderhearted guy, anyway!

"We led worship with it that night," Scott recalls. "It was a powerful time."

Scott soon changed the name from the "Fisherman's Song" to "Take My Life."

"I know people call it 'Holiness,' because it's the first line of the song," he says, "but I called it 'Take My Life' because it seemed like it best described the gist of the song. I know that line isn't even in the piece, but it describes what the song is about."

After appearing first on Scott's groundbreaking 1995 *Hallelujah Glory*, the song has since made its way onto several other Vineyard recordings and dozens of independent projects. Its popularity has scaled any fences that might separate the Vineyard movement from the larger church; it's become a favorite across denominational lines.

Scott is also appreciated broadly for such praise songs as "You are God," "You Are in Control," and "Another Drink." "Take My Life," however, currently has the broadest reach.

Although raised in a Christian home, Scott says that a pastor, Sam Sasser, influenced his young heart to focus on worshiping God.

"I didn't realize what a foundation he had laid in me until later," says Scott. "Sam had been a missionary in the Marshall Islands, and his whole platform of ministry was praise and worship. I don't recall a message when he *didn't* talk about praise and worship."

As a boy, Scott also deeply experienced the impact of pop hits from the 1970s.

"My older brothers came home with a song by the Guess Who, and I just loved it," he says. "I remember [Simon and Garfunkel's] 'Parsley, Sage, Rosemary and Thyme,' listening to it and staring at the album cover. It did something to me. I was engulfed by the melodies.

"When I was little, I'd go to my grandparents' church with my parents. When the piano would start to play, I'd start to cry . . . so much that my grandfather would have to take me out of the room! The Lord had really made my heart sensitive to the power of music."

Although he had a childhood conversion to Christianity, Scott spent some years distant from God. He rededicated his life to Christ in 1983, and soon married Donna, his former teen sweetheart.

The Underwoods's lives have since been characterized by worship leading and church planting. "If I'm traveling anywhere and she's not with me it's very tough," Scott says candidly. "Donna and I have always been a team. When I've done recordings for the Vineyard, she's sung with me; it would be hard to do it without her."

Two daughters and a son are following in their footsteps. "We've lived in Belfast for six months and visited India this summer. I know the Lord is raising them up to do wonderful things."

Until recently, Scott was worship pastor at San Luis Obispo Vineyard Christian Fellowship, but he is currently Director of Worship Development at Vineyard Music Group.

"My heart is to encourage worship leaders to focus only on Him and to direct people's attention to Him and take the pressure off themselves to come up with a slick performance. Though it's good to play your instrument well, the important thing is to put people's attention, affections, and focus on the Lord.

"Songs become important only if you choose the wrong one; the song becomes the focus only when it's not working. In some songs, either the focus isn't right, or it might not be totally scriptural, but it doesn't have the effect of bringing us into the presence of God.

"I don't want to put an inflated importance on songs. But I do want to use the songs that I know are going to bless Him and help us worship Him."

26

There Is None Like You

LENNY LEBLANC

"I got on my face and started weeping. . . . I couldn't believe that God was that good to give me something that great."

Some people would give anything for a recording contract with one of the world's largest and most influential music labels. Lenny LeBlanc gave up his recording contract so that he could truly have everything.

He had a lot to give up. Throughout the 1970s, Lenny had been a successful pop artist, his career hitting some especially impressive peaks toward the end of the decade.

Then in 1981, Lenny got a call from a close friend who lived in Florida.

"He was a big-time drug smuggler," says Lenny. "He called me late one night and said, 'Lenny, I got saved. I'm going to heaven, and I want you to be there with me. Are you saved?' This friend was like an older brother to me, so what he said had weight. I thought, *Oh, man, this is great. Now that I'm successful and have all this stuff going for me, he starts talking about God.* I had no idea what *saved* even meant. I hadn't been inside a church in probably twenty years. And the church that I'd gone to as a child never talked about salvation, so I didn't know anything about it. He sent me a Bible, and I started reading, and God started revealing Himself to me."

As the words on the page spoke into Lenny's life, he found himself torn up about choices he'd made in the past. "I was just eaten up with guilt because I'd left my family six or seven years before that for my career. God started revealing to me how I was in need of Him. His love melted my heart. I started crying out to God for forgiveness, and I became born again right there in my house."

Lenny's friends suggested that he might be losing his mind. "They thought I was nuts, that I was going off on some religious tangent, but I'd found the Lord."

At that time, Lenny was signed to Capitol Records as a solo artist and had one record left on his contract. As he sat down to write songs for that record, praise and worship—not pop lyrics—fell from his lips.

"Every time I'd write a song, by the time I got to the chorus it would be about what Jesus had done in my heart. I called my manager in Los Angeles and said, 'Do you think they'd let me out of my record deal?' He thought I was completely crazy."

Crazy or not, Capitol Records agreed to put Lenny in suspension of his contract—he couldn't record for another label unless they bought out his contract. This was unlikely, since Christian music was still a relatively small industry in 1981. Few Christian record labels could afford to buy Lenny away from Capitol.

Forced into an early retirement from the music industry, Lenny—a talented craftsman as well as musician—made stained glass. Often he'd get a job creating a window for a church, and the church would ask him to give his testimony to the youth group, sing a song during the Sunday morning service, or give a Saturday night concert. At the same time, Lenny was still writing. But his songs were no longer about worldly matters. They were about the things of God. By the time Lenny had written more than a dozen Christian songs, God began to open new doors.

Lenny soon met many of the key figures in Christian music, including Michelle Pillar, who recorded three of his tunes. Two years after he left Capitol Records, Capitol realized that no one was willing to purchase Lenny's contract. They let him out of the agreement. Now Lenny recorded his own albums, this time for smaller Christian labels. But industry shake-ups and financial considerations at the labels often interfered with his releases, leaving a sour taste in Lenny's mouth.

"I got really frustrated with the whole industry," Lenny says. "I thought, *This is the kind of stuff that goes on in pop music.* All these Christian artists wanted to cross over to pop music, and I was saying, 'Wait a minute. You don't want to go there. You don't want to go there!'"

Finally, in 1986, Lenny pulled back from the music industry and turned his focus to leading worship at his home church in Florence, Alabama. There, he noticed a need for more strong praise and worship music.

"Back then we were singing camp meeting songs," he says. "We really didn't have any contemporary worship songs. I started asking God, 'Would you give me some songs, just for our home fellowship? You know, songs that will relate to our generation?' And so I started writing worship songs."

Lenny met some of the leaders at Maranatha! Music, and they started using some of his songs—as well as his voice—on their projects. In 1990, Lenny recorded a solo worship album for Maranatha! He also provided background vocals on more than twenty of Integrity Music's Hosanna albums, and the label started using several of his songs on various projects. In the early 1990s, Integrity approached him about doing a worship CD for them. When Lenny sat down to write a collection of songs specifically for that project, 1994's *Pure Heart*, "There Is None Like You" was born.

"I had a deadline and had to write ten songs, or at least three or four great songs that would eventually make it to the CD. So one morning I began playing the piano. A lot of times, I'll just hum along with the piano, with no real idea to write about. Or I'll sing words that don't make any sense to anyone else, but I'm trying to stir up an idea. But that morning I started singing, 'There is none like you. . . .' It just built from there, and another line or two came for the chorus."

After he had completed the chorus, Lenny took a brief break and thought, *Wow, this could really be something good.*

"I went back into the studio and I sat down at the piano and sang through the chorus a few more times and fine tuned it. And that's when the weight of it hit me—that it was a wonderful song and it was going to have a huge impact all over the world. I got on my face and started weeping. I couldn't control it. I couldn't believe that God was that good to give me something that great.

"Then I started writing the verse, and the verse took me down, too. I was ruined. So, it was just a weeping morning."

After the success of *Pure Heart*, Integrity signed Lenny as a solo artist, and he spent time writing songs that were not specifically worship songs. "But even when I wrote the artist-type songs," he says, "they were always written from a heart of praise."

For four or five years, Lenny wrestled with the dilemma, What am I? Am I an artist? Am I a worship leader? Although highly skilled and successful in both roles, Lenny ultimately felt the strongest calling in the area of worship.

"The second line of 'There Is None Like You' says, 'No one else can touch my heart like You do.' That's where God touches us—in our hearts, in our spirits, and nobody else can do that like He does. There's thousands of ways in which there's none like Him, but that's the one way I wanted to convey: 'No one else can touch my heart like You do. I could search for all eternity long and find that there is none like You.'

"No person, no thing, no amount of money, no fame. I don't care what you put up against it, it doesn't even hold up."

Story approved by Lenny LeBlanc. "There Is None Like You" by Lenny LeBlanc, © 1991, Integrity's Hosanna! Music/ASCAP, c/o Integrity Media, Inc., 1000 Cody Road, Mobile, AL 36695.

27

You Are My Hiding Place

Michael Ledner

"It felt like any other song. I had a sense of, 'Oh, that might be a nice song.'"

A t twenty-seven years of age, Michael Ledner was completely on fire for God. He was also separated from his wife of nearly ten years.

At this painful time in his life, Michael relied more heavily than ever on a creative outlet that had served him since his teenage years—songwriting.

Married at age eighteen, right out of high school, they remained legally wed for close to a decade but he was separated from his wife for the last two years of their relationship. In 1980—living in a rented seven-by-ten-foot room in a house in Tucson, Arizona—he often turned to the Scriptures for comfort and inspiration.

One evening, Michael sat on his bed with his guitar in hand, the Scriptures lying open before him, experimenting with different verses and songs. He came upon a part of Psalm 32:7, "You are my hiding place." He then remembered a phrase from Psalm 56:3, "When I am afraid I will trust in you." Immediately, Michael decided to tie those two thoughts together.

> *You are my hiding place.*
> *You always fill my heart with songs*
> *of deliverance, whenever I am afraid.*
> *I will trust in you, I will trust in you.*
> *Let the weak say I am strong in the strength of the Lord.*

"*Voila,*" he says today. "I wrote the song! Within one or two hours, it was done." At the time, Michael didn't realize the impact the song would have.

"It felt like any other song. I had a sense of, 'Oh, that might be a nice song. Oh, well.' And I recorded the song, put the guitar away, and went to sleep."

It's ironic that the song's last line, which was also pulled from Scripture, was taken somewhat out of context. Because, now a pastor, Michael says, "I'm a real stickler when it comes to making sure we understand the words we're singing and that they are, indeed, used in context, the way they were intended."

At the time, however—despite immersing himself in Scripture and memorizing verses for years—Michael drew the concept, although not the exact context, from the Bible.

"I remembered the passage that contained the literal words, 'Let the weak say I am strong.' But it wasn't 'in the strength of the Lord.' I thought that's what it meant when I wrote the song. I'd probably heard some person wrongly teach that. The verse [Joel 3:10] actually says 'Let those weaklings say they are strong!' of the people who were coming against Israel.

"When somebody pointed that out to me, I remembered what Paul said in Second Corinthians: 'When I'm weak, I'm strong.' That's what I *really* meant!"

Cutting straight to the emotions of worshipers, the song did not suffer the slightest from that initial contextual confusion.

Not long after writing the song, Michael shared it with a couple of friends, and the three sang it together while he made a new recording. After they'd finished, Michael thought once again, "Oh, that's a nice song." He then put the tape on a shelf and abandoned it for nearly a year.

"I would be in congregations where I could share songs, but I didn't do anything with *that* song," he says. "It had some words that I felt were kind of corny—not real manly. It says 'hiding,' 'afraid,' and 'weak'—stuff that men really *love*. I felt like it was too vulnerable."

During this period, though, Michael wasn't aware of the nature of his emotions. "I was just trying to figure out, 'Why didn't I share that song? It's a nice song.' I was still working through being separated and, soon after, divorced."

While cathartic, writing the song brought him face to face with some of the most agonizing of human emotions.

"It was a song that said 'I'm hiding. I'm afraid and I'm weak.' Later, I realized that strong men of God, like Paul and Moses and David, hid and were afraid and were weak. We will *all* hide and be afraid and weak. What's important is what we do with that. When I'm afraid, I can go to the Lord, or I can deny it, or I can run to something other than the Lord. And when I'm weak, I can try to do something in my own strength to make me feel strong, or in weakness I can go to the Lord and really be strong in Him."

Eventually, Michael says, he realized, "Hey, it's very honest and good and manly, even, to sing that."

Nine months after writing the song, Michael was in Israel with a group that had volunteered to serve on a communal settlement known as a *kibbutz*. One night, he came across the tape of "You Are My Hiding Place," which he had recorded with his two friends. Since the meeting was about to begin, Michael thought, *Oh, I guess I'll share this tonight.*

He did, and several friends who were visiting learned the song and took it back to the United States, where they sang it in Vineyard Christian Fellowship and Calvary Chapel congregations in California.

Not long afterward, Michael, who was still in Israel, received an unexpected phone call from executives at Maranatha! Music. They wanted to record "You Are My Hiding Place" for their *Praise 6* album.

"It's pretty cool to get a phone call from the States when you're in Israel," he says. "Especially from a record company that's been singing your song and wants to get your permission to publish it!"

Today, "You Are My Hiding Place" continues to win the hearts of people of all ages, from all countries.

"It has such volatile words in it that people quickly identify with it," Michael observes. "It seems to immediately endear me to people; it's like they're saying, 'You hit it!' People identify with hiding in the Lord. They identify with fears and they identify with being weak. . . . It's just so human. In our humanness we connect to God."

Following the painful years of his separation and divorce, Michael traveled with the Liberated Wailing Wall, a musical touring group with Jews for Jesus. He then studied at Multnomah Bible College and Seminary and later became a pastor. He currently pastors at a Foursquare Gospel church in Scottsdale, Arizona, and enjoys a successful marriage with Lylah, to whom he has been married for over a decade.

Both his personal life and ministry benefit today from the lessons he learned so many years ago.

"When a person goes through a divorce, there are great feelings of rejection," he says. "Many times, a person isn't even aware of these feelings. I wasn't. 'You Are My Hiding Place' was a shot in the arm to me. It gave me confidence to move out in gifts that God had given to me, and it taught me not to be the final judge of the creative things I do."

Michael hopes his story will encourage those who are reluctant to use their creative gifts in the church.

"I say to people, 'A lot of times your creative work is going to be so close to home that you don't want to share it. Don't be the judge of that. If God stirs you to share something, even if it's a total flop, that doesn't mean *you're* a flop. You're not a good judge of your own stuff because you're too close to it. Just get it out and don't worry about the results.

"Don't be like this guy who waited nine months because he felt like it was corny."